...rmediate

English for
BUSINESS LIFE

IAN BADGER   PETE MENZIES

Self-study guide

Marshall Cavendish
Education

Acknowledgements

The authors would like to thank the following for their great help and advice in the preparation of *English for Business Life*: Simon Ross, Lucy Brodie, Jo Barker, Graham Hart and Teresa Miller.

We would also like to thank our business 'students' from organisations including UPM-Kymmene Oyj, Metso Paper, BEMIS, Peterson Packaging, Vattenfall, the International Maritime Organisation, GE Finance, ABN Amro (Investment Bank), Dresdner Kleinwort Wasserstein (UK), Matsushita Europe and Marketing Akademie Hamburg for providing the inspiration and feedback that underpins *English for Business Life*.

Marshall Cavendish ELT
119 Wardour Street
London W1F 0UW

Designed by Hart McLeod, Cambridge

Printed and bound by Times Offset (M) Sdn. Bhd. Malaysia

Photo acknowledgements

Pg 5 l Photo Network / Alamy r Iconica, Pg 8 Comstock Images / Alamy, Pg 11 Corbis, Pg 13 Uppa, Pg 16 image100 / Alamy, Pg 19 Paul Box, Pg 22 Stock Connection Distribution / Alamy, Pg 24 Rex, Pg 26 Iconica, Pg 28 PCL / Alamy, Pg 30 Iconica, Pg 32 Kim Kulish / Corbis, Pg 34 Alamy Pg 36 Uppa, Pg 39 Photos12, Pg 42 Design Pics Inc / Alamy, Pg 45 Imagestate, Pg 47 NASA / Corbis, Pg 50 Andy Bishop / Alamy, Pg 52 Peter Bowater / Alamy, Pg 54 Iconica, Pg 56 Rex, Pg 59 Iconica, Pg 61 Iconica, Pg 63 Retna, Pg 65 Empics, Pg 67 Rex, Pg 69 Ace Stock Limited / Alamy, Pg 71 Reuters / Corbis, Pg 74 tl Sean Potter / Alamy, tr Sean Potter / Alamy, bl Pixonnet / Alamy, br Picturesbyrob / Alamy, Pg 76 Rex, Pg 78 Corbis, Pg 81 Photonica, Pg 84 Vottoriano Rastelli / Corbis, Pg 86 Image Source / Alamy, Pg 88 Rex,

Contents

Introduction

The Self-study guide is part of the *English for Business Life* business English course. It follows the *English for Business Life* syllabus and language programme. Each level of the *English for Business Life* course has a Self-study guide – this is the pre-intermediate level.

This Self-study guide can be used:

- as a stand alone self-study course
- in class to supplement *English for Business Life* course work
- for homework
- as a key component of the 'comprehensive' study track (the *English for Business Life* course has three study tracks: fast, standard and comprehensive)
- as practice material for learners who are following general English courses and need practice in everyday business English.

Each unit begins with a recorded summary of useful phrases and includes:

- clear study notes
- realistic practice exercises.

At the back of the guide are:

- an easy-to-follow language reference section
- a glossary of key business-related terms
- clear answers and audioscripts to support the practice exercises.

The recorded material is available on a CD which is included with the book. The recordings include standard accents and examples of people from different parts of the world speaking English.

Recommended study procedure

- Listen to the Useful Phrases as often as possible and repeat where appropriate.
- Work through the Study Notes and refer to the Reference Section as indicated.

- Note down words and phrases that are particularly useful to you.
- Use a good dictionary to check the meanings of unfamiliar words.
- Work through the exercises and then check the answers at the back of the book.

Some study tips

- Approach language learning with the same level of commitment that you would any other project in your work. It can be useful to prepare a 'contract' with yourself in which you agree to do a certain amount of work on your English per day/week/month.
- In our view, 'little and often' is more effective than occasional long study sessions. When you travel, take your Self-study guide with you. You can work with it at times that suit you – for example, when you are in your car, at home or on a plane. Journeys can provide a great opportunity for uninterrupted practice.
- Use new language and phrases whenever possible. Live practice is the best way to learn new terms.
- Keep a paper/electronic study file in which you note down the language most relevant to your everyday needs.
- Relate the language presented and practised to your particular area of business. If there are terms you need which are not included in the material, do some research on the Internet, and consult English-speaking colleagues, friends and teachers.
- Make use of the English-speaking media – in particular facilities on the Internet. Listen to the radio and TV. Read professional journals and newspapers. Subscribe to an English magazine which interests you from a work or leisure point of view.

UNIT 1

You and your background

Some useful phrases

Listen to the recording and repeat

My name is Tom Sand.
I work for the MAX hotel group.
I studied accountancy at university.
I have a degree in business studies.

Which department are you in?
I am (I'm) in the administration department.
I'm in Admin.
Do you work in the personnel department?
Yes, I do.   No, I do not (don't).

What do you do?
I'm an administrator.
　　a sales executive　　a technician

I'm the managing director.
I'm the chief accountant.

Where are you from?
Where do you live?
Where do you come from?
I come from London.
I was born in London, but I live in Zurich.

Are you married?
No, I'm not. I'm single.
　　single　engaged　divorced　separated

Do you have any children?
I have a son and a daughter.
How many children have you got?
I've got two sons.

Study notes

I work for …

Note these other examples:

What do you do?　　　　*Does your company make …?*
I live in Berlin.　　　　*I don't live in Geneva.*

See also Reference Section 2.1 for details of the Simple Present tense.

A degree in business studies.

Notice also these qualifications:
a BA (bachelor of arts) in business studies
an MSc (master of science) in engineering
a diploma in industrial design

I'm in Admin.

Note that a capital letter is used for names of departments.
I'm in Sales, Accounts, etc.
Compare with: the administration department.
Admin = administration.

Are you married?

We can say:
He married last year.
or *He got married last year.*

See also Reference Section 20.7.

I have a son and a daughter.

Notice these terms:

husband	*wife*	*partner*
boyfriend	*girlfriend*	
son-in-law	*daughter-in-law*	
father-in-law	*mother-in-law*	

How many children have you got?

Have you got in the present tense is more common in UK English.
Do you have is more common in US English.

Practice

Some nationalities and cities

1 Listen to the recording. Match the people with where they work.

a	An Italian	**i**	the Paris office
b	A Scot	**ii**	the Cairo office
c	An American	**iii**	the Tokyo branch
d	An Egyptian	**iv**	the Munich office

Prepositions

2 Fill the gaps in the dialogues with an appropriate preposition.

A: What do you do?

B: I'm an IT manager. I'm responsible **a** .....*for*...... all information systems **b** .... the office.

A: Who do you work **c** .... ?

B: A company called Root Chemicals. I've been **d** .... them **e** .... two months.

C: What qualifications do you have?

D: I have a degree **f** .... engineering.

C: Where did you go **g** .... college?

D: I went **h** .... the Berlin Institute **i** .... Technology.

E: Where are you **j** .... ?

F: Algeria. My parents are French, but I was born **k** .... Tangiers.

Vocabulary

3 Complete the vocabulary sets, using words from the box.

brother-in-law	football	college	clerk ✔
married	engineering	university	certificate
data processing	father-in-law	production	diploma
separated	law	tennis	executive ✔

e.g. manager	...*clerk*.......	...*executive*.....
a single	....	....
b mother-in-law	....	....
c golf	....	....
d school	....	....
e administration	....	....
f degree	....	....
g accountancy	....	....

Questions and answers

4 Write answers to these questions. Then write a paragraph about yourself.

a Who do you work for?

....

b What do you do?

....

c Where do you work?

....

d How do you travel to work?

....

e Where are you from?

....

f Where do you live?

....

g Do you like it here?

....

A personal profile

5 Read the text and answer the questions.

Tori Westman is our new HR manager. She was born in Sydney, Australia. Before joining MCT, she was with the Telco group, where she was responsible for the payroll and management information systems. She is 28 years old and engaged to Robert Redmaid, a systems analyst with Kettle and Forbes. Tori has a degree in business and communications.

a Where did Tori work before joining MCT?

....

b What is her job at MCT?

....

c How old is she?

....

d What does her fiancé do?

....

e What was she responsible for at Telco?

....

f What qualifications does she have?

....

UNIT 2

Company structure

Some useful phrases

Listen to the recording and repeat

I work for AMT.

We are (We're) based in London.

Our main business is telecommunications.

We have offices in Manchester and Glasgow.

offices   branches   subsidiaries

I am (I'm) in the oil business.

the IT business	electronics
pharmaceuticals	packaging
furniture	construction

We are (We're) a limited company.

a public company   a partnership

What does PLC stand for?

It stands for 'public limited company'.

We employ 220 people.

We have a staff of 50.

The head office is in London.

We are a subsidiary of the DAB group.

Our parent company is DAB.

Our managing director is on the DAB board.

Who is in charge of purchasing?

Who is the person above him?

Who does he report to?

Who is his line manager?

What is his job title?

His job title is CEO.

He's also the production director.

Maxine runs the Portuguese plant.

She is (She's) also responsible for our Spanish operations.

Study notes

Notice that the pronunciation of *the* changes from /ðə/ before a consonant (the DAB group) to /ðiː/ before a vowel (the oil business).

I work for AMT.

Notice that *the* is not normally used with company names: IBM, Sony, Coca-Cola, etc. But when the name ends with *company* or *corporation, the* is needed: *the* Sony Corporation, *the* Coca-Cola Company, etc.

We're a limited company.
a public company

A limited company is a company with limited liability. A public company is a limited company which can sell shares and securities to the public. For these and other business-related terms, see also the Glossary, pages 118–122.

What does PLC stand for?

Notice these abbreviations: PLC (public limited company), Ltd (limited), Inc (incorporated), Co. (company), CEO (chief executive officer).
See also Reference Section 22.16 for a list of other common abbreviations.

the head office
a subsidiary

Revise the use of articles (*a, an* and *the*).
Note the following examples:
She is a lawyer. (not *She is lawyer.*)
I work for a company called CST Engineering.
(not *I work for company called …*)
Business is good. (not *The business is good.*)
They make cars. (not *They make the cars.*)
See also Reference Sections 11.1 and 11.2.

the Portuguese plant

See Reference Section 22.12 for a table of countries and nationalities.

Practice

Names of industries

1 Listen to the recording and match the employees to the main business of their companies.

a A maintenance supervisor
b A systems analyst
c An office manager
d A production manager

i Hotels and travel
ii Mining
iii Clothing
iv Computer software

Articles (a/an, the)

2 Write *the*, *a* or *an*. Some sentences do not need an article.

e.g. I work in .....*the*..... dairy industry. We sell dairy products. We have .....*a*.... subsidiary in France.

a I'm in .... Sales.
b I work in .... marketing department of a company that sells electrical products.
c I'm not .... boss.
d We sell direct to .... supermarkets.
e I'm .... employee.

f We have .... offices in the UK, Italy and Portugal.
g We sell .... margarine, ... milk and .... yoghurt.
h We have .... processing plant in Normandy.
i My boss is .... accountant.
j When I was in Paris, I visited .... Pompidou Centre and .... Eiffel Tower.

A company organisation chart

3 Complete the sentences about the diagram.

e.g. The person ....*above*.... Marc Vicario is Joe Roger.

a Ivan Cluff .... for finance.
b .... runs the production side.
c Debbie Murphy is in charge of ....
d .... Rex Took, there are three managers.
e Kurt Malkin reports to ....

Norman Packaging PLC organisation chart

f .... is responsible for

....

g .... is in charge of

....

h .... reports to

....

Explaining your position in a company

4 Answer the questions about yourself. Then read the example statement and write a paragraph about yourself.

a Who do you work for?

....

b What business are you in?

....

c What kind of company is it?

....

d Are you part of a group?

....

e Who is the head of the company? What is his/her job title?

....

f Where is your head office? Where are you based?

....

g Which department are you in? Who runs it?

....

h How many people does the company employ?

....

I work for a medium-sized limited company. We are in the financial services business. The company is based in Madrid. Our CEO is Manuel Alhunìa. We have offices in Europe and South America. We employ 200 people. I am the senior marketing manager. I report to Roberta Lazar, the sales director. I have twenty sales reps under me.

Nationalities

5 Complete the phrases.

e.g. (USA) a *n American* switchboard operator

a (Holland) a .... MD

b (France) a .... sales manager

c (Germany) a .... human resources manager

d (Belgium) a .... accountant

e (Hungary) a .... office manager

f (Poland) a .... technician

g (Brazil) a .... marketing manager

h (Japan) a .... sales executive

i (Scotland) a .... receptionist

j (China) a .... trainee accountant

UNIT 3

Company history

Some useful phrases

Listen to the recording and repeat

When was the company founded?

It was founded in 1971.

It was set up by John Smith.

It was based in Scotland.

We moved our head office to Geneva in 1989.

The company expanded in the 1990s.

    the seventies   the eighties   the nineties

We employed 500 people.

We took on new staff.

We bought a US manufacturer in June 1989.

An office was opened in France.

Production was started in Spain.

When was that? What was the date?

It was the spring of 1991.

    spring   summer   autumn   winter

It was at the beginning of the month.

    at the beginning

    in the middle

    at the end

Alpha took us over in 2001.

We were taken over in May.

Was the engineering division sold off?

    sold off   closed down   cut back

Yes, it was.   No, it was not (wasn't).

I joined the company in 2005.

    I left after the takeover.

40 people lost their jobs.

Study notes

When was the company founded?

We form the Past Passive tense by combining the Past tense of the verb *to be* (*was/were*) with the Past Participle (*founded*).

The Past Participle of regular verbs is the same as the Simple Past.

See Reference Section 21 for a list of irregular verbs.

in 1971

Note the prepositions in dates and times:

in 1987, in June, on Monday, at 3pm.

See also Reference Section 19.1.

We moved our head office …

Revise the Simple Past tense.

See Reference Section 2.5.

in the 1990s

Notice the following:

the 90s = the nineties

the 1980s = the nineteen eighties

in the early/late nineties

in the mid-seventies.

We took on new staff.

Take on is a phrasal verb, a verb in two parts. Note that we can say:

We took on new staff.

or *We took new staff on.*

I left after the takeover.

Here are some verbs that are used as nouns:

Verb	Noun	Verb	Noun
to merge	*a merger*	*to increase*	*an increase*
to acquire	*an acquisition*	*to decrease*	*a decrease*
to take over	*a takeover*	*to close (down)*	*a closure*
to expand	*expansion*	*to sell (off)*	*a sale*
to produce	*production*	*to grow*	*growth*

Practice

Milestones

1 Listen to a speaker talking about the history of a company run by his uncle. Write down what happened on these dates.

e.g. 1960s *The leather factory in Minneapolis was set up.*

1982 ....

1983 ....

1986 ....

1995 ....

1997 ....

2004 ....

Now ....

Simple Past tense

2 Put the verbs in brackets in the Simple Past tense.

e.g. (*drive*) I ......*drove*...... to work this morning.

a (catch) I .... the bus yesterday.

b (wear) I .... my new suit.

c (buy) I .... some sandwiches for lunch.

d (spend) I .... the whole day in the office.

e (write) I .... some letters.

f (get) I .... home at 6.15.

Vocabulary

3 Change the sentences by using the noun form of the underlined words.

e.g. The old plant was <u>closed down</u>.
The ......*closure*...... took place at the end of last year.

a We <u>merged</u> with EDU in 1997.

The .... was a disaster.

b We <u>acquired</u> a sales company in Peru.

It was an important ....

c We were <u>taken over</u> last year.

The .... was very successful.

d We <u>expanded</u> our sales force in the spring.

This .... was essential.

e The number of complaints <u>decreased</u> last year.

The .... was not expected.

Prepositions of time

4 Fill in the gaps with prepositions of time.

e.g. We were taken over ....*at*........ the end of July.

a I'm meeting her .... 4pm .... the 25th.

b He resigned .... Easter.

c I'll see you .... lunchtime.

d The company was set up .... 1989.

e The company was closed .... the middle of June.

f We are very busy .... February.

Examples of the passive

5 Write the sentences in the passive.
e.g. John Smith set up the company in 1985.
The company ...*was set up in 1985*...... .

a He bought a factory in the States in 1997.
A factory ....

b We acquired our Japanese subsidiary in 1999.
Our Japanese ....

c We closed the American factory in 2004.
It ....

d ZRF took us over in 2005.
We ....

e They pulled down the original factory.
The original factory ....

UNIT 4
Current projects

Some useful phrases

Listen to the recording and repeat

What are you working on at the moment?

I am (I'm) working on a project in the Middle East.

It is (It's) for a large packaging company.

You do (do you do) a lot of work in the Middle East?

We are (We're) designing a new computer system.

We're installing a security system.

We're building a new warehouse.

We build a lot of warehouses.

How is it going?

It's going well.

It is not (isn't) going very well.

We're planning to start next week.

We're hoping to finish by the end of June.

The project is on schedule.

We're two weeks ahead of schedule.

We're two months behind schedule.

We're having problems.

We're still working on stage one.

What is (What's) the problem?

We cannot (can't) get qualified programmers who can speak English.

> qualified   experienced   skilled
> English   Japanese   French   German

Will you complete on time?

> I hope so.

Are you going to finish behind schedule?

> I hope not.

Study notes

What are you working on at the moment?
We're designing a new computer system.
The Present Continuous tense is used for actions and situations that are happening at the time of speaking:
I am talking to John.   *It is raining.*
See also Reference Section 2.2.

Do you do a lot of work in the Middle East?
Note the use of *do* in these expressions:
to do business   *to do the accounts*
to do the paperwork   *to do the cleaning/typing*
See also Reference Section 20.2.

We build a lot of warehouses.
Revise the Simple Present tense. Can you answer these questions?
What does your company do?   *Where do you work?*
What do you do in the evenings?
See also Reference Sections 2.1 and 2.3.

behind schedule
Schedule is often pronounced /ʃedjuːl/ in UK English, and /skedʒʊl/ in US English.

... who can speak English.
Revise the names of languages. In most cases, the word is the same as the adjective of nationality.
He speaks French.   I live in France.   He is French.   It is a French car.
Note that the names of languages plus nationalities are written with a capital letter.

... I hope so.
Notice these phrases:
I think so.   *I don't think so.*   *I think not.*
I hope so.   *I hope not.*
I believe so.   *I believe not.*
See also Reference Section 16.4.

Practice

Work in progress

1 Listen to the managing director of a consultant engineering company describing three projects that his company is involved in. Complete the information.

a | PROJECT FOR: hydro electric power station
COUNTRY:
SCHEDULE: three weeks ahead of schedule
START-UP:

b | PROJECT FOR: brewery
COUNTRY:
SCHEDULE:
START-UP:

c | PROJECT FOR: effluent treatment plant
COUNTRY:
SCHEDULE:
START-UP:

Progress report

2 Read the email and fill in the gaps. Rewrite the email for a client or customer, putting in your own details.

ahead of	going well	I am writing ✔
I think	skilled	is going
the end of next week	working on	

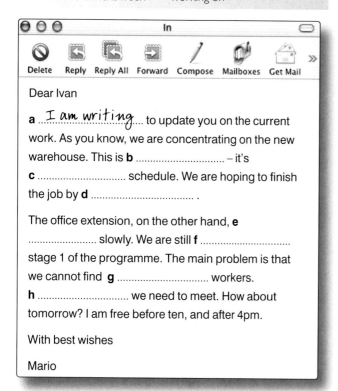

Dear Ivan

a ...I am writing.... to update you on the current work. As you know, we are concentrating on the new warehouse. This is **b** .... – it's **c** .... schedule. We are hoping to finish the job by **d** ....

The office extension, on the other hand, **e** .... slowly. We are still **f** .... stage 1 of the programme. The main problem is that we cannot find **g** .... workers.

h .... we need to meet. How about tomorrow? I am free before ten, and after 4pm.

With best wishes

Mario

Present Continuous vs. Simple Present tense

3 Write sentences using the correct form of the Present tense.

e.g. (you/like) the plans for the new warehouse?

...... Do you like the plans for the new ......
...... warehouse? ......

a How (it/go)?

....

b (you/speak) German?

....

c What (they/work/on) at the moment?

....

d (we/build) a lot of warehouses like this.

....

e (I/not/know) your email address.

....

f (I/not/think) we will finish on schedule.

....

g (we/want) to start work on the project next month.

....

Prepositions

4 Find another way of saying these phrases by writing prepositions in the gaps.

e.g. She's having a holiday.

… ....*on*.............. holiday.

She's …

a … having a meeting.

… .... a meeting.

b … travelling to Moscow.

… .... her way to Moscow.

c … having lunch.

… .... lunch.

d … working in the office.

… .... work.

e … entertaining some customers.

… .... some customers.

f … playing golf.

… .... the golf course.

A personal statement

5 Read the paragraph and answer the questions. Then write a paragraph about one of your current projects.

> I work for a large packaging company, based in Belgium. We sell a range of packaging materials. We do most of our business in Northern Europe. At the moment, we are working on a big order for FTZ, a Norwegian company. We are also trying to increase our sales in the American market. I'm currently working on some samples for a customer in Detroit.

a What business is she in?

....

b What does the company sell?

....

c Where do they do most of their business?

....

d What are they working on at the moment?

....

e What are they trying to do?

....

f What is her current project?

....

UNIT 5

Meeting a visitor

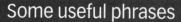

Some useful phrases

Listen to the recording and repeat

Excuse me, are you Miron Golek?

I am (I'm) here to meet you.

We are (We're) here to take you to your hotel.

My name is Sandy Wonham. This is Lisa Blom.

How do you do?

Pleased to meet you.

Can I introduce Joe Dorf?

Do you know Joe?

Yes, we have (we've) met.

Hello. Welcome to London.

How are you?

I'm fine.

How are your family?

They're very well.

It is (It's) good to see you again.

It is (It's) good to see you too.

How was your journey?

Did you have a good flight?

It was fine.   It was awful.

It was not (wasn't) very comfortable.

Was the plane on time?

Yes, it was.   No, it was not (wasn't).

Is this your luggage?

No, that is (that's) mine.

Whose is this briefcase?

It does not (doesn't) belong to me.

Study notes

This is Lisa Blom.

Note the following introduction:

May I introduce Mrs Smith?   *May I introduce myself?*

I'd like you to meet our publicity assistant.   *Do you know Mary?*

How do you do?

This is not a real question. It is used in introductions. The formal response is to repeat the question:

A: *How do you do?*   **B:** *How do you do?*

Other possible responses are *Pleased to meet you* and, less formally, *Hello*.

Hello. Welcome to London.

Note the times when the following are used: *Good morning* (till lunchtime), *Good afternoon* (from lunchtime till about 5pm), *Good evening* (for the rest of the night till midnight). *Good day* is used in some areas, including Australia. *Good night* is a farewell, not a greeting.

It's good to see you again.

Notice the use of the infinitive (*to see*) in this construction. Note these other examples:

It's nice to meet you.   *It's good to talk to you.*

Is this your luggage?
No, that's mine.

Revise possessive adjectives (*your, my,* etc.) and possessive pronouns (*yours, mine,* etc.).

See Reference Section 13.2.

Whose is this briefcase?

Note these uses of *whose*:

Whose bag is this?   *Whose is this (bag)?*

See Reference Section 16.1 for other question words.

It doesn't belong to me.

Revise object pronouns (*me, us,* etc.).

See Reference Section 13.1.

Practice

Meeting a visitor

1 Listen to the recording and complete the dialogue. Then listen again and repeat.

A: a .....*Excuse me,*..... are you Otto Ringer?

B: Yes, I am.

A: Hello, my name is Jan Reemik. This is Don Wallis. We're from CET.

B: b .... ?

C: c ....

A: d .... London. We're here to meet you and take you to your hotel.

B: e ....

A: It's our pleasure. How was your flight?

B: f ....

A: g .... ?

B: Yes, it was.

C: Are these your bags, Mr Ringer?

B: Yes, they are.

C: h .... ?

B: i ....

A: Right, the car park is this way.

Arrangements to meet a plane

2 Complete the email by filling in the gaps. Then write your own version for a visitor you might meet.

booked	confirm	flight
hope	meet ✓	Regards
satisfactory	seeing	take

```
 ○ ○ ○                          In                        ▭
  ⊘        ↩         ↩        →       ✎        📫        ✉    »
Delete   Reply   Reply All  Forward  Compose  Mailboxes  Get Mail

Dear Sergio

I will a ......*meet*...... the 10.30 b ..................... from
Rome on the 23rd April, and c ....................... you to
your hotel. I have d ....................... you into the
Columbia Hotel. I e ....................... that is OK. Your
first appointment is at 2.30pm. Could you please
f .............................. that these arrangements are
g ........................... ?

I am looking forward to h ....................... you again.

i .......................

Richard White
```

whose

3 Write the questions. Then write possible responses.

e.g. Whose/bags

  – Whose are these bags?
  – They're mine.

Who/wallet

  – Who does this wallet belong to?
  – I thought it was yours.

a Whose/briefcase

  – ....

  – ....

b Who/keys

  – ....

  – ....

c Whose mobile phone

  – ....

  – ....

d Who/laptop

  – ....

  – ....

e Whose/papers

- ....
- ....

f Who/glasses

- ....
- ....

g Who/security pass

- ....
- ....

h Whose/gloves

- ....
- ....

Possessive adjectives and pronouns, and object pronouns

4 Complete the statements as shown.

e.g. This is John's case.

[1] *And this is his too.*

or [2] *And this is his case too.*

or [3] *And this belongs to him too.*

a These are my bags.

[1] ....

b This is Mary's luggage.

[2] ....

c This is our table.

[1] ....

d This is Mr Krinol's suitcase.

[3] ....

e These are my children.

[3] ....

f This is Mrs Dikrop's security pass.

[1] ....

g These are our drinks.

[3] ....

h These are your tickets.

[1] ....

Commenting

5 Complete these sentences, using the verb *to be* and the words in the box.

delicious	slow	comfortable	high
on time ✓	excellent	poor	quick
useful	good	fast ✓	helpful

e.g. The flight ..*was on time*.., but the bus connection ..*wasn't fast*..

a The food .... , but the service
....

b It .... trip, but the weather
....

c The hotel .... , but the staff on reception ....

d The queue for the check-in .... , but passport control ....

e Their facilities .... , but their prices
....

UNIT 6

Introducing your home town

Some useful phrases

Listen to the recording and repeat

Excuse me, can you give me a lift?
Of course, where do you want to go?

Is it your car?
No, it is (it's) a company car.

What is (What's) it like?
It's reliable and economical.
It's easy to drive.
There is (There's) lots of room.

This is the cathedral.
That is the town hall.
The museum is behind those buildings.
The university is over there.

> police station   post office   hospital
> town hall   chamber of commerce
> library

There is an industrial park on the outskirts of the city.
Are there good rail links with Europe?

> Yes, there are.   No, there are not (aren't).

There used to be more heavy manufacturing.
There was a ferry service, but it closed down.
Were there warehouses along the river?
Yes, there were.   No, there were not (weren't).

What's the population?
Twelve thousand five hundred.
Two hundred and fifty thousand.
One point two million.

Study notes

... can you give me a lift?
Note also these phrases:
Could you take me to …?   Could I come with you?

What's it like?
Notice also these questions:
What is your boss like?   What is your car like?
What is the weather like?   What is your office like?
We can reply to these questions with a description (*He's tall and wears glasses*) or an opinion (*He's very nice*).

There's lots of room.
Lots of is an alternative to *a lot of*. Both can refer to singular or plural nouns:
There is a lot of room.   There are a lot of cars.
There are lots of cars.
See also Reference Section 15.4.

This is the cathedral.
That is the town hall.
The museum is behind those buildings.
Revise the use of *this, that, these* and *those*.
See also Reference Section 14.

There is an industrial park ...
Revise the use of *there* with the verb *to be* (*is/are/was/were*):
Is there an airport?   *There aren't any facilities.*
There was a problem with their order.   *Were there any calls?*
See also Reference Section 1.2.

There used to be more heavy manufacturing.
Note the negative and the interrogative of *used to*:
Did there use to be …? (not *Did there used to be …?*)
See also Reference Section 20.9.

Practice

Driving to the hotel

1 Listen to the dialogue and fill in the gaps.

A: Excuse me. Can you ..*give me a lift*.. ?

B: Yes, of course. Where are you going?

A: To my **a** .... I'm staying at the Imperial.

B: That's no problem. I'm going that way …

B: Do you see that place over there?

A: Yes.

B: That's the new **b** .... , which opened last summer. It's very **c** .... There used to be a glass factory there, but it was pulled down.

A: What are those buildings?

B: The first one is the **d** .... , and that's the main library …

A: … Is that the **e** .... ?

B: Yes, that's right. The train service to Geneva is excellent, and there are good links to **f** .... from the airport.

A: What's the population?

B: It's just over **g** .... , I think.

Numbers

2 Write the numbers in words.

e.g. 407 ......*four hundred and seven*..............

a 407,000 ....

b 300 ....

c 2,100 ....

d 1,099 ....

e 1,105 ....

f 143,280 ....

g 147m ....

h $11\frac{3}{4}$m ....

Demonstratives (this, these, etc.)

3 Write *this*, *these* or *those* in the blanks.

e.g. Are ...*those*... documents on the table over there confidential?

a .... is John. I'm calling from New York.

b What are .... on the table?

c Who was .... man?

d Are .... your keys on the floor by the door?

e Here, could you give .... note to Rosario?

f They are coming .... afternoon.

g Is .... your boss over there?

h Who said .... ?

i Who are .... people in the car park?

j Is .... Zenith Ltd [on the phone]?

there is/are
there was/were
there used to be

4 Compare the sentences using *is*, *are* (*not*) or *used to be*.

e.g. There ...*used to be*..... factories along the river, but they were pulled down.

There ......*are*......... houses there now.

a There .... any shoe shops in Sturgot Road now. There .... two near the library, but they closed down two years ago.

b There .... a bread factory in Djamba Square, but it went out of business.

c There .... a new industrial park on the outskirts of town.

There .... a farm there before.

Now write examples about your town area.

d There is/isn't ....

e There are/aren't ....

f There was/wasn't ....

g There used to be ....

City profile

5 Read the city profile. Then write questions for the answers. Write a brief profile of your city or town.

Haranga is 115 kilometres from the capital, in the north-east of the country. The town has a population of 960.000. The main industries are banking and insurance, aircraft construction and food processing.

There used to be more heavy manufacturing. There were many factories and warehouses in the industrial part of the town, south of the River Droat. Many of these are now closed. Today, the city is a centre for high-tech industry and financial services. There are good rail and road links with major commercial and industrial centres. The nearest airport is in Granton, 27 kilometres away.

The town has a fine cathedral and a theatre. There used to be a zoo, but it closed two years ago. There are three cinemas.

e.g. It's 115 kilometres from the capital, in the north-east of the country.
..................Where is Haranga?..................

a 960,00

b Banking and insurance, aircraft construction and food processing.

c There used to be, but many of the factories and warehouses closed.

d They are good. There are links with major industrial and commercial centres.

e The nearest airport is 27 kilometres away in Granton.

f Yes, there is. It's a very beautiful building.

g Two years ago.

h Three.

a ....
.... ?

b ....
.... ?

c ....
.... ?

d ....
.... ?

e ....
.... ?

f ....
.... ?

g ....
.... ?

h ....
.... ?

UNIT 7
Chance meetings

Some useful phrases

Listen to the recording and repeat

Hello. What a surprise!
How nice to see you!

How are you?
How is (How's) business?
How's your family?
You are (You're) looking well.

It is (It's) good to see you (again).
How long have you been here now?
How long are you staying?
Are you here on business?

    on business   on holiday

What are you doing these days?
Are you still working for Zenith?

Where are you staying?
At the Hilton hotel.

Give me a ring some time.
We must meet for lunch.
Here is (Here's) my card.

I am (I'm) afraid I have to go now.
Remember me to your boss.
Give my regards to your wife.
Say 'hello' to John for me.

Goodbye.   Bye.
See you soon.   Good night.

I have (I've) just seen Tony Kwon.
He has (He's) gone now.
You have (You've) just missed him.

Study notes

What a surprise!
Revise the use of *how* and *what* (*a*) in exclamations.
How wonderful.
What a great opportunity.
See also Reference Section 20.15.

How long have you been here now?
Notice that the question in this situation is not *How long are you here now?*

Give me a ring some time.
Revise the use of imperatives. Note that *please* can be used:
Please remember me to your wife.
See Reference Section 7 for notes on the use of imperatives.

We must meet for lunch.
Must can be used in invitations:
You must come to lunch.   *You must visit us.*
You must bring your wife.   *We must have a game of tennis some time.*

I'm afraid I have to go now.
It is also possible to say *I must go*. *Must* and *have to* are similar in meaning.
See also Reference Section 9.3.

Bye.
Goodbye is often shortened to *Bye*. *Good night* is a farewell; the greeting is *Good evening*.

See you soon.
Revise farewells. *See you soon* is short for *I will see you soon*. It is more informal. Note also:
See you later.   *See you tomorrow.*   *See you on Wednesday.*

I have (I've) just seen …
Revise the Present Perfect tense.
Note that in US English, the Simple Past is often used instead of the Present Perfect.
See Reference Section 2.8.

Practice

Greetings and goodbyes

1 Listen to the recording and match the speakers with what they say.

   a An American banker.
   b A Scottish businesswoman, friend.
   c An Australian.

   i We must keep in touch.
   ii Thanks for a wonderful evening. Good night.
   iii Give my regards to your wife.

Short exchanges

2 Match the questions with the responses.
   e.g. How's business?   iii

   a How's your family?   ☐
   b How long have you been here?   ☐
   c What are you doing these days?   ☐
   d Are you still working for Zenith?   ☐
   e Remember me to your boss.   ☐

   i I'm working for a company called Zudeck.
   ii They're fine.
   iii Not bad. How's business with you?
   iv I will. See you soon.
   v No, I've got a new job.
   vi About seven months.

how, what *and imperatives in courtesies*

3 Fill in the gaps.
   e.g. ....*Remember*.... me to your wife.

   a Do .... her my best wishes.
   b .... hello to James for me.
   c .... him to give me a ring some time.
   d .... us know if there's a problem.
   e.g. ....*How*.... nice to see you!
   e .... a disaster!
   f .... a beautiful day!
   g .... strange!

A chance meeting

4 Fill in the gaps in the dialogue using the words and phrases in the box.

   good   must   on business   still   these days   what ✔

   A: Hello, ...*what*.... a surprise! How are you?
   B: I'm very well, thanks. **a** .... to see you.
   A: And you. What are you doing **b** .... ?
   B: I'm **c** .... working for TLK.
   A: Are you here **d** .... ?
   B: Yes, we have an office here now.
   A: Listen, we must meet for lunch some time.
   B: Yes, we **e** .... I'll call you.

The Present Perfect tense

5 Write sentences using the Present Perfect tense.
   e.g. – (hear/the news?)
       ....*Have you heard the news?*....
     – The President is dead.

   a – (I/just/see/John)
      ....
     – Really? Where is he?

   b – Where are your friends?
     – (They/go)
      ....

   c – I'd like to speak to Mr Smith.
      ....
     – (you/just/miss/him)

   d – (How long/you/be/married?)
      ....
     – About six years.

UNIT 8
Shopping

Some useful phrases

Listen to the recording and repeat

I am (I'm) looking for a pair of trousers.

    trousers   socks   gloves   glasses

I need a couple of shirts.

What size are you?

Can you tell me what size you are?

    Small.   Medium.   Large.

What is (What's) your waist size?

    waist   collar   sleeve   chest   leg

My collar size is $16\frac{1}{2}$ inches.

Can you measure it?

What's that in a European size?

These are too small.

The sleeves are not (aren't) long enough.

Have you got a larger pair?

Have you got them in cotton?

    cotton   wool   silk   nylon   polyester

How much are they?

They are (They're) 90 euros.

I cannot (can't) afford that.

Have you got anything cheaper?

What's that in dollars?

How many dollars are there to the euro?

Do you take Visa?

    credit cards   dollars   cash

They are (They're) fine.

They fit perfectly.

I will (I'll) take them.

Study notes

a pair of trousers
Note these examples of when we use *a pair of*:
a pair of glasses, a pair of shoes, a pair of socks, a pair of trousers, a pair of gloves, a pair of tights, a pair of earrings.
Note that *some* can be used in the place of *a pair of*:
some trousers, some shoes, etc.
Note that *trousers = pants* in US English.

I need a couple of shirts.
Note that *a couple* means approximately two.
Check that you know this other common clothing vocabulary:
jacket, coat, raincoat, suit, tie, belt, shirt, blouse, skirt, dress, scarf.

Can you tell me what size you are?
Revise indirect questions. Note the word order:
How much is it?   *Can you tell me how much it is?*
When there is no question word, we use *if* or *whether*:
Do they sell hats?   *Do you know if/whether they sell hats?*

$16\frac{1}{2}$ inches
One inch = 2.54 centimetres. Many English-speaking areas, including the States, use inches, feet, miles, etc. Note that metre (UK English) = meter (US English) and centimetre (UK English) = centimeter (US English).
See also Reference Section 22.9.

These are too small.
The sleeves aren't long enough.
Revise *too* and *not enough*. Note these examples:
too long, too quickly   *big enough, efficiently enough*
enough time, enough chairs   *Is there enough?*
We didn't buy enough.
See also Reference Section 15.4.

Buying a pair of shoes

1 Listen and write the questions. Then listen again and repeat.

A: a .... ?

B: I'm looking for a pair of formal black shoes.

A: b .... ?

B: Seven.

A: What's that in European size?

B: I'm not sure.

A: I'll check … You need a size 39. These are your size.

B: c .... ?

A: They're €120 a pair.

B: d .... ?

A: It's about 150 US dollars.

B: e .... ?

A: f .... ? They're €105.

B: g .... ?

A: Of course … They suit you.

Shopping vocabulary

2 Arrange these words in sets.

trousers	extra large ✓	supermarket	collar
wool	newsagent	jewellery	gloves
chest	small	sleeve	medium
flowers	polyester	perfume	shoe shop
tights	nylon		

a large   *extra large*   ....

b cotton   ....

c waist   ....

d socks   ....

e chocolates   ....

f chemist   ....

too, enough

3 Put the words in the right order.

e.g. waist/enough/the/big/is

.... *Is the waist big enough?* ....

a big/don't/they/make/clothes/enough

....

b too/me/it's/for/small

....

c tight/shoes/me/too/are/these/for

....

d don't/enough/we/have/time

....

e busy/now/I'm/to/do/too/it

....

Indirect questions

4 Write indirect questions or statements for the following responses, using *Can you tell me*, *Do you know* or *I need to know*.

e.g. – *Can you tell me what size you are?*

   – I'm medium.

a – ....

   – Yes, I want it in blue.

b – ....

   – No, I'm afraid that is the biggest one we have.

c – ....

   – Yes, these are cheaper.

d – ....

   – No, I'm afraid we don't have it in cotton.

e – ....

   – It's 5,000 roubles.

UNIT 9

Health problems

Some useful phrases

Listen to the recording and repeat

How are you feeling?

I've got a headache.

I think I have (I've) got a temperature.

temperature	sore throat
cold	cough

What is (What's) the matter?

What's wrong (with you)?

My stomach hurts.

I've got a bad back.

I've got a pain in my chest.

head	arm	leg
heart	neck	shoulders

I am (I'm) not sleeping well at the moment.

I'm under a lot of pressure at work.

I'm feeling awful.

tired	ill	sick	dizzy

Where is (Where's) the first aid box?

Do you have any paracetamol?

There is (There's) some antiseptic cream in the cupboard.

There are some pills on the shelf.

plasters	bandages

You should take some time off.

He ought to be in bed.

She should see a doctor.

We ought to call an ambulance.

He does not (doesn't) look very well.

He should not (shouldn't) be at work.

Study notes

I've got a headache.
Note also these common health problems:
(*a*) *stomach ache*, (*a*) *toothache, a sore throat, flu.*

My stomach hurts.
Notice that parts of the body are normally used with a possessive adjective (*my, your,* etc.):
I have hurt my leg.   *She has got a pain in her neck.*
Notice that *stomach* is pronounced /ˈstʌmək/.

I'm feeling awful.
Notice that the verb *feel* can be used in the Simple Present or the Present Continuous tense with no change of meaning. This is also true of *look* and *hurt*:
You look well.   *My head hurts.*
or *You are looking well.*   **or** *My head is hurting.*
See also Reference Section 2.3.

Do you have any paracetamol?
There's some antiseptic cream in the cupboard.
Revise the use of *some* and *any*.
See also Reference Section 15.1.

… paracetamol?
Note this common first-aid vocabulary:
pain-killer, antibiotic, bandage, plaster, cotton wool.
Note these verbs used for accidents:
cut, burn, fall, slip, hit, bang.

You should take some time off.
He ought to be in bed.
Revise the forms of *should* and *ought to*. They are used when giving advice:
She should see a doctor.   *He ought to go home.*
See Reference Section 9.4.

Practice

Saying what is wrong

1 Listen to the recording and complete the table.

SICK LIST			
Name	**Department**	**Complaint**	**Date**
Dwight Grey	PR	cold/sore throat	14/03
Claude Lupo	Catering	burns (left hand)	26/03
Mary Sudetic	Sales	migraine	27/03
Dan Orbach	**a**	**b**	30/03
Ken Pole	**c**	**d**	6/04

Vocabulary

2 Complete the vocabulary sets with words from the box.

tired	ear	call off	paracetamol ✓
cold	dentist	sore throat	healthy
shoulder	pain-killer ✓	doctor	well
nose	cancel	run down	neck

e.g. aspirin *paracetamol* *pain-killer*
a back ....
b eye ....
c postpone ....
d cough ....
e nurse ....
f worried ....
g fit ....

should, ought to

3 Give advice using *should/shouldn't* and *ought/oughtn't to*.

e.g. I've got a terrible headache.
.... *You should go home.* ....

walk on it	go home ✓
go to hospital	be at work
see a doctor	put something on it

a Tom's got a bad back.
....

b My shoulder hurts.
....

c Miss Morello has a pain in her leg.
....

d My secretary cut her finger.
....

e John Brett has burnt his hand rather badly.
....

some, any

4 Fill in the gaps using *some* or *any*.

A: What's the matter?

B: I need some cotton wool. Have you got ...*any*...?

A: What happened?

B: I fell and cut my knee.

A: Yes, you must clean that. I'll get **a** .... from the first aid box.

B: Could you also get **b** .... antiseptic cream?

A: There isn't **c** .... – well, there wasn't **d** .... last week when someone needed **e** ....

An email saying you are unwell

5 Write an email using the phrases provided.

I'm afraid – my doctor – to stay in bed – and a high temperature – has advised me – I have a bad cold

I'm sorry – at work – any inconvenience – on the 21st – on my mobile – if this causes you – you can contact me – I should be back

UNIT 10

Location and layout

Some useful phrases

Listen to the recording and repeat

How do I get to your office?
It is (It's) in the centre of town.

    in the suburbs
    on the outskirts of town

We are (We're) on an industrial estate.

We're just outside the city centre.

… eight miles to the south of the centre.

… five kilometres north-east of the centre.

    north-west   south-west   south-east

Come off the motorway at Junction 10. Turn left at the traffic lights.

    at the crossroads   at the roundabout

Take the second turning on the left.
Do not (Don't) take the first on the right.
Follow the signs to the motorway.
Drive through the village.

My office is opposite the garage.
It's next to the engineering works.
The reception desk is by the main entrance.
My office is on the second floor.
Take the lift to the third floor.

Which building is the warehouse?
It's the one with the scaffolding.

    with the red roof   with the low roof

It's the building with no windows.

Study notes

How do I get to your office?
Note the use of *get* here. You can also say:
Can you tell me the way to your office?

in the centre …
… on an industrial estate.
My office is opposite the garage.
See Reference Section 19.2 for more on prepositions of place.

We're eight miles to the south of …
We're five kilometres north-east of …
Note that 1 mile = 1.609 kilometres.
See Reference Section 22.13 for points of the compass.

Come off the motorway …
Drive through the village …
See Reference Section 19.3 for more examples of prepositions of direction.

Turn left at the traffic lights.
Revise these words connected with driving:
roundabout junction turn-off motorway main road crossroads

Take the second turning on the left.
Don't take the first on the right.
Note these examples of imperatives used for directions.
Note also that we normally use the contracted form *Don't go* (not *Do not go*) when we give directions.
See Reference Section 7 for more information on imperatives.

… on the second floor.
second floor (UK English) = third floor (US English)
first floor (UK English) = second floor (US English)
ground floor (UK English) = first floor (US English).

Take the lift to the third floor.
Lift = elevator in US English.

Directions

1 Listen to the speakers and make a note of the directions they give.

'How do I get to your office?'

a A British businessman
b An American workshop manager
c A Chinese sales director
d A Scottish management consultant
e A German agrochemicals consultant

Prepositions of direction

2 Fill in the gaps using the words in the box.

to	up ✓	from	after	back to
past	under	through		

Go a ...*up*.... the hill. when you come b .... the top, turn left. Go c .... a garage, and d .... a railway bridge. You'll soon come to a small village. Drive e .... the village. Just f .... the village you'll see the first signpost to the motorway. If you get lost, go g .... the village and start again h .... there.

Imperatives

3 Look at the map, then complete the directions by adding verbs in the imperative. Note that the traffic is moving on the left.

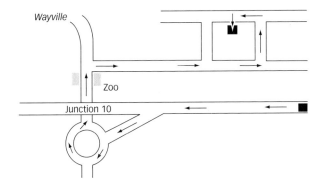

Take the motorway going west and a ......*follow*...... the signs to Wayville. b .... the motorway at Junction 10. As you come off, you come to a roundabout. At the roundabout c .... right and go under the motorway. d .... along that road until you come to some lights. The sign says that Wayville is straight on, but e .... straight on; f .... right. g .... past the zoo, which is on your right, then, h .... the first turning on the left (it's a no-entry). i .... the second turning. j .... down to the end of that road and then k .... left. Our office is about 300 metres further on, on the left.

Prepositions of place

4 Look at the diagram and fill in the gaps with prepositions.

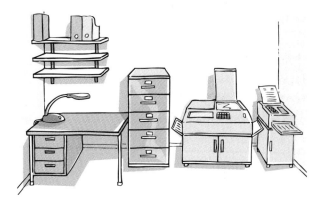

a The lamp is ......*on*.... the desk.
b The desk is .... the filing cabinet.
c The filing cabinet is right .... the photocopier.
d The filing cabinet is .... the desk and the photocopier.
e The shelves are .... the desk.

UNIT 11

The people you work with

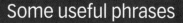
Can I speak to someone in Accounts?

Is there anyone who can help me?

Can you tell me who deals with invoice enquiries?

Could you tell me something about the people who work in production?

Who is (Who's) in charge of production?

Fernando Rex is our production manager.

He organises the work shifts.

He is (He's) responsible for industrial relations.

Does he have to liaise with the sales department?

What else does he do?

Who does he report to?

He reports to the technical director.

Who plans the production programmes?

Do you?

No, that is not (that's not) my job.

I do not (don't) have to do that.

That is (That's) the production planner's job.

I look after the northern sales area.

Ron Dix covers the south.

Do you subcontract any work?

No, we do not (don't).

Study notes

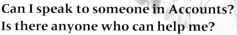

Practise saying the following words:

north /nɔːθ/	*northern* /ˈnɔːðən/
south /saʊθ/	*southern* /ˈsʌðən/
west /west/	*western* /ˈwestən/
east /iːst/	*eastern* /ˈiːstən/

Can I speak to someone in Accounts?
Is there anyone who can help me?

See Reference Section 15.3 for more on *someone* and *anyone*. Note also:

finance	*production*
administration	*sales*
purchasing	*HR (Human Resources)*
IT (information technology)	*logistics*

Who's in charge of production?
Who does he report to?

Note that *To whom does he report?* is outdated.
See Reference Section 16.1 for more on *who* as the subject and object of a sentence.

… in charge of production.
He's responsible for industrial relations.

Note the expressions *in charge of* and *responsible for*.

Does he have to liaise with the sales department?
I don't have to do that.

liaise with = work with, cooperate with
See Reference Section 9.3 for further details of *has/have to* and *doesn't/don't have to*.

That's the production planner's job.

Note the informal use of *job* in this example.

Practice

Jobs

1 Listen and write down what each speaker's job is.
   a An English man ....
   b A German man ....
   c A French woman ....
   d A Russian man ....

has/have to

2 Complete the sentences with *have/has to do* or *don't/doesn't have to*.
   a I'm glad I ..... *don't have to* ..... go out tonight. I'm very tired.
   b I'm sorry, but I .... leave now.
   c I .... change any money. I've got plenty left from my last trip.
   d Pedro .... organise the work shifts any more.
   e Who .... (you) see tomorrow?

Vocabulary

3 How many combinations can you make with the words below?

production	deputy	department	section
sales	senior	manager	director
assistant	accounts	administrator	office

a production manager   *the sales section*

....

who

4 Write a question in reply to the first statement.
   e.g. I sent a message to the Swedish office.
   ..... *Who did you send it to?* .....
   To Christel Berglund.

a I got a letter from one of our engineers.
   .... ?
   It was from Brian Toms.
b I left a parcel in reception.
   .... ?
   The security guard.
c I heard yesterday that we have a new MD.
   .... ?
   The technical director told me.
d I work closely with the production manager.
   .... ?
   He has to liaise with the shift supervisor.

someone, anyone

5 Write *anyone/anybody* or *someone/somebody* in these sentences.
   a Can I speak to .... in the production department, please?
   b .... from your sales department called.
   c Does .... know what is happening?
   d If you have a problem with an invoice, ask .... in Accounts to help you.
   e I don't know .... in the accounts department.

Questions

6 Write questions using the prompts.
   e.g. (who – in charge of – customer service?)
   ..... *Who is in charge of customer service?* .....
   a (he – be – with the company – long?)
   .... ?
   b (where – he – work before?)
   .... ?
   c (which company – he – work for?)
   .... ?
   d (who else – work – here?)
   .... ?

UNIT 12

A tour of the premises

Some useful phrases

Listen to the recording and repeat

Welcome to Sarco Aerospace.
I'd like to welcome you all to Sarco.
I hope everyone had a good journey.
I would (I'd) like to tell you something about the company.
Then I will (I'll) show you round the plant.
Do you have any questions?

This is the sales section.
The conference room is over there.
My office is at the end of the corridor.
Those stairs lead to the testing area.
There are more offices upstairs.

This map shows the whole site.
You came in here.
On this site, we have a production plant, an administration block and a warehouse.

We are (We're) now walking past the testing area.
Would you like me to show you the warehouse?

> warehouse   storage area
> main laboratory

Yes, I would.   Thank you.

Do you mind if I smoke?
Not at all.
Do you mind if we look in here?
I am (I'm) afraid you cannot (can't).
It is (It's) private.

Be careful.   Mind your head.
Do not (Don't) touch that. The paint's wet.
Mind where you walk. It's slippery.

Study notes

I'd like to welcome you all to Sarco.
I hope everyone had a good journey.
Some other 'welcoming' phrases:
It's nice to see you here.   Please make yourselves comfortable.
I hope you (all) had a good journey.

I'd like to tell you something about …
Note the use of *I'd like to* in these examples:
I'd like to welcome you to Sarco Aerospace.
I'd like to show you this map.

Would you like me to show you the warehouse?
Notice also:
I want you to …   I'd like you to …
(We do not say *Would you like that I show you the warehouse?*)
See also Reference Section 20.5.

Do you mind if I smoke?
Not at all.
Do you mind if we look in here?
I'm afraid you can't. It's private.
Notice the question *Do you mind if …?* and the responses.

Be careful.
Mind your head.
Don't touch that.
Mind where you walk.
Imperatives are used for warnings in the affirmative and negative.
Note also:
Mind your back.   Mind your eyes.   Hold on (tight).

The paint's wet.
It's slippery.
Note also:
It's very steep.   It's very high.   It's very low.
It's very dirty.   It's greasy.   It's sticky.

Practice

A welcoming talk

1 Listen to the extracts from a talk welcoming visitors to an aerospace company. Are the statements true ☐T☐ or false ☐F☐?

a The speaker does not want the visitors to take their jackets off. ☐

b The company started on its present site in 1925. ☐

c The factories are concentrated in one part of the country. ☐

d Wings will be built in Bulgaria in the future. ☐

e There will be no time to look in the hangars. ☐

Do you mind …?

2 Write sentences with *Do you mind …?* Then write responses.

e.g. Let's sit down here.
- <u>Do you mind if we sit down here?</u>
- <u>No, not at all.</u>

a Can I open the door?
.... ? ....

b Is it OK if I have a cigarette?
.... ? ....

c Can I post the letter tomorrow?
.... ? ....

d Is it OK if I leave early?
.... ? ....

e Would it be OK to look in here?
.... ? ....

Imperatives for warnings

3 Match the two parts of the warnings.

a The floor is very dirty. ☐i☐

b Don't touch that door. ☐

c These stairs are steep and slippery. ☐

d The ceiling is very low. ☐

e Watch out for that electric cable. ☐

i Mind where you walk.
ii Be careful. Hold on to the rail.
iii It's live.
iv The paint is wet.
v Mind your head.

Would you like me to …?

4 Rewrite the sentences with *Would you like me to …?* or *I'd like you to …* . Then write possible responses.

e.g. Shall I call you?
- <u>Would you like me to call you?</u>
- <u>Yes, that would be a good idea.</u>

a Shall I send it by fax?
b Shall I post it for you?
c Can I show you anything else?
d Tell me something about the company, please.
e Could you book a table for me?
f Please be very quiet.
g Can you show me the testing area?

Showing someone round

5 Who would say the following:
- the visitor? ☐v☐
- the company representative? ☐CR☐

a Is this the warehouse? ☐v☐

b Is this your office? ☐

c Is this your first visit to the company? ☐

d How many fork-lift trucks do you have? ☐

e Have you been round a bottling plant before? ☐

f Where do you store the empty bottles? ☐

g How many shifts do you work? ☐

UNIT 13
Graphs and charts

Some useful phrases

Listen to the recording and repeat

Let me show you this graph.

pie chart	bar chart
diagram	table

It shows our sales by market area.

Sales reached a peak in 2002.

2002 was a very good year for us.

They fell to their lowest point in 2004.

Prices have been stable for years.

We have (We've) reduced the size of our workforce …

… since last year.

… in the last five years.

Business has gone badly in recent years.

Ten years ago, business was good.

Do you sell much to Japan?

What percentage of the total goes to Japan?

Japan accounts for 75% of our deliveries.

They buy three-quarters of our production.

It was 10% two years ago.

Production has increased …

… dramatically.

… slightly.

… by slightly more than 7.5%.

(by seven point five per cent)

(by seven and a half per cent)

Profit was 5% up on last year.

Study notes

Notice the pronunciation of *-age* in *percentage* /pəˈsentɪdʒ/

by market area
Note also the use of *by* in: *by geographical area.*

Prices have been stable for years.
Note also:
Prices have been stable since last year.
Prices have been stable in recent years.

… in the last five years.
We can also say: *in the past five years.*

Business has gone badly …
Production has increased dramatically.
Note the use of *badly* and *dramatically*.
See Reference Section 18 for more about adverbs.

Ten years ago, business was good.
Notice the use of *since, in, ago* and *for* here.
See also Reference Section 20.11.

What percentage of the total goes to Japan?
Notice this question.
(We do not say *How many per cents go to Japan?*)
Note also these questions:
What percentage (of your deliveries) does Japan account for?
What percentage does Japan represent?

Japan accounts for 75% …
They buy three-quarters of our production.
See Reference Section 22 for details of percentages and fractions.

Production has increased by … 7.5%.
Notice the use of *by* in this example.

Profit was 5% up on last year.
Note also:
Sales were down on the previous year.

Practice

Using a pie chart/percentages

1 Listen to the recording and fill in the information on the pie chart.

Main customer areas

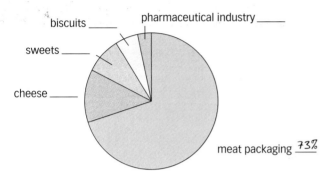

biscuits _____
pharmaceutical industry _____
sweets _____
cheese _____
meat packaging _73%_

Adverbs

2 Complete the sentences with a suitable adverb.

quickly	hard	easily	slowly
extremely ✓	slightly	recently	

e.g. I'm _extremely_ sorry.

a It rained very .... last night.

b You speak English very ....

c I can't understand you very ....

d Could you speak more .... ?

e We have .... increased our prices by 2%.

f We have had a lot of problems ....

Expression of time

3 Write sentences about yourself and/or your company.

e.g. _We have reduced the size of our workforce_
in recent years.

a .... three months ago.

b .... since this morning.

c .... for the last fifteen minutes.

d .... in recent months.

e .... since the beginning of last year.

f .... two days ago.

Vocabulary/phrase

4 i How many combinations can you make from the words in the box?

pie	vertical	horizontal
bar	graph	sales
chart	annual	axis

e.g. ...... _pie chart_ ....

....

ii Match the phrases to make sentences.

a They have increased prices   **i** a peak in 2005.

b Let me show you   **ii** 20% of our exports.

c Sales reached   **iii** by less than 2%.

d Prices remained   **iv** stable last year.

e 5% of our production goes   **v** to the Far East.

f South America accounts for   **vi** this graph.

Fractions and percentages

5 Write the fractions and percentages in words.

e.g. $\frac{3}{8}$ _three-eighths_ ....

a $3\frac{1}{4}$ ....

b $\frac{1}{8}$ ....

c $\frac{3}{4}$ ....

d $\frac{1}{3}$ ....

e 4% ....

f 21.5% ....

g 0.6% ....

UNIT 14

Profit and loss

Some useful phrases

Listen to the recording and repeat

Did you make a profit last year?

We made a profit of £5 million.

Most of our branches made a profit.

Some of them made a loss.

One branch lost $3.5 million.

Turnover has increased.

   increased   decreased   fallen

Profit fell last year.

This has been a good year.

Last year was a bad year.

Have you seen this year's accounts?

   balance sheet   profit and loss account

Who audited the accounts?

Who are your auditors?

We had to borrow a lot of money last year.

We now owe the banks a lot of money.

We have large bank loans.

We are £500,000 in debt.

The bank is our biggest creditor.

Expenditure was €½ million over budget last year.

Did you take on many new people?

Did you spend much on furniture?

We spent a lot of money last year.

We lost a lot of money on the project.

Study notes

Notice that the *b* in *debt* is silent. /det/

Turnover has increased.
Profit fell last year.
Do you know this vocabulary?

turnover	*profit*	*loss*	*budget*
credit	*debt*	*expenditure*	*audit*
auditor	*balance sheet*	*profit and loss account*	

This has been a good year.
Last year was a bad year.
Have you seen this year's accounts?
Who audited the accounts?
Note the contrast between the Simple Past and Present Perfect tenses.
See also Reference Section 2.7.

Who audited the accounts?
Who are your auditors?
Note these groups of words and check you understand what they mean.

an auditor	*an audit*	*to audit*	*a creditor*	*a credit*
to credit	*a debtor*	*a debt*	*to debit*	

Expenditure was €½ million over budget …
Notice that *budget* can be used as a verb or as a noun:
We have spent this year's budget.
We have budgeted for expansion.

Did you take on many new people?
Did you spend much on furniture?
We spent a lot of money last year.
Note these examples of *much, many* and *a lot of*.
See also Reference Section 15.4.

We lost a lot of money on the project.
Note that we can *make* or *lose* money *on* something.

Practice

Business performance

1 Listen to the speakers talking about the performance of their business. Give marks for performance as follows:

5 – very good	2 – good and bad
4 – good	1 – bad
3 – quite good	0 – very bad

'How was business last year?'

a An Austrian IT manager ☐

b An American marketing manager ☐

c A Danish CEO ☐

d An American sale executive ☐

e An Indian senior administrative manager ☐

Simple Past and Present Perfect

2 Complete the sentences with a suitable form of the verb in brackets. Use the Present Perfect where possible.

a If we look at the whole year there ..*has been*.. (be) a rise in profits.

b But turnover .... (decreased).

c Profits .... (be) down sharply in March …

d … but they .... (rise) in April.

e … and they .... (end) this year well up.

f We .... (recently) (repay) a £5 million loan to the bank.

g Things .... (get) even better.

h The bank .... (offer) to extend our overdraft facility.

i We .... (become) very optimistic about the future.

Perfect Present tense

3 Tick ☑ the sentences where the Present Perfect (*has/have done*) is also possible.

a Did you check the ledger? ☑

b I checked the ledger this morning. ☐

c When were the accounts last audited? ☐

d They were audited last month. ☐

e We received the money. ☐

f We received the money last week. ☐

g I called your clerk yesterday. ☐

h She was very busy this morning. ☐

i Did you speak to our credit controller? ☐

j Did you meet our accountant when you were in Lima? ☐

k No, I met her in Quito, when I was in Ecuador. ☐

much, many, a lot (of)

4 Complete the sentences with *much*, *many* or *a lot* (*of*). In some cases, there is more than one possibility.

e.g. **A:** Did you make .....*much*....... money last year?

B: No, not **a** .... It was a bad year.

A: Did you take on **b** .... new people?

B: No, not **c** ....

A: We took on **d** .... new staff. But we don't need so **e** .... this year. We have closed down **f** .... of our offices. There's not **g** .... of our European business left.

B: How **h** .... business do you do in the States?

A: i ....

Financial statement

5 Fill in the gaps using the words in the box.

creditors	price	bank loans
healthy ✓	debts	corner
expenditure	market conditions	

Last year was a very good year for us. The balance sheet has never been so **a** _healthy_ . We managed to pay off nearly all of our **b** .... , and to clear all of our other **c** .... Our **d** .... have finally stopped chasing us for money! The main reason for all this was the dramatic decrease in the **e** .... of our raw materials and the excellent **f** .... in Europe last year. Consequently, profit was 20% over budget, and **g** .... was well down on what it was the year before. We feel that we have now turned the **h** .... , and we expect next year to be even better than this year.

Comparing turnover

6 Read the text below and complete the analysis of the comparing turnover.

ANALYSIS OF TURNOVER	CURRENT PERIOD: 3 months to 31.3 (€m)	LAST YEAR: 3 months to 31.3 (€m)
Road haulage	400	....
Boat building	....	....
Furniture	....	....
Supermarkets	....	....

This year to March has been a mixed one for us. Turnover has increased in the road haulage and boat building industries, but the supermarket sector hasn't performed well and our furniture business has been a disaster. If I can give you the figures: in the three months to March 31st, turnover in the road haulage business was €400 million, compared with €388 million the previous year. Boat building was up from €60 million to €63 million this year. The bad news is furniture; down from €378 million to €362 million and supermarkets from €220 million to €213 million.

UNIT 15

Invoicing and payment

Some useful phrases

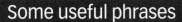

Listen to the recording and repeat

Can I talk to your credit controller?

    your accountant   your bookkeeper

Can I speak to someone in …

… the accounts department?

… the purchasing department?

… the sales department?

What are your payment terms?

We ask for 30 days net.

You can pay weekly or monthly.

Can we pay by monthly instalments?

We would prefer regular monthly payments.

Can I pay by bank transfer?

Which currencies do you accept?

Does the bill include sales tax?

What is (What's) the tax rate?

You need to add VAT at 18%.

Could you send me an invoice?

I will (I'll) send you one immediately.

I'll send you a cheque in two days.

Payment was due two months ago.

We have not (haven't) received the transfer.

Did you receive the money?

No, we did not (didn't).

You will (You'll) have the money tomorrow.

You have (You've) invoiced us for ten chairs.

We only ordered five.

Study notes

the purchasing department
Note also:
purchase ledger department   *sales department*   *sales ledger.*

What are your payment terms?
We ask for 30 days net.
Can we pay by monthly instalments?
Notice these expressions for terms of payment.

We would prefer regular monthly payments.
We can say:
either *We receive payments monthly.*
or *We receive payments every month.*
But we must say:
We receive monthly payments.
(not *We receive every month payments.*)

Does the bill include sales tax?
Bill is an informal word for *invoice.*

You need to add VAT at 18%.
Note these mathematical terms:
Add the VAT.   *Subtract the VAT.*
Multiply the total by six.   *Divide the total by four.*
2 + 2 = 4 (*two plus two equals/makes four*)
4 − 2 = 2 (*four minus two equals/makes two*)

I will (I'll) send you one immediately.
You will (You'll) have the money tomorrow.
Note the use of *will* for sudden decisions and promises.
See also Reference Section 3.4.

Payment was due two months ago.
Notice these other expressions with *payment*:
to make a payment   *to delay payment*   *to ask for payment*
to demand payment

A missing invoice

1 Listen and answer the questions. Then write a brief note for Mr Kloss's file, summarising the call.

a Who is calling who?

....

b What is the reason for the call?

....

c What is the background situation?

....

d What is the specific problem?

....

e What action has been agreed?

....

....

....

A reminder letter

2 A client has not paid. Put the sentences in this letter into the correct order.

Dear Sir

If you have already paid this invoice, please disregard this letter.

Could you please transfer the money as soon as possible.

This was due four weeks ago.

We have not yet received payment of our invoice number 12239.

Yours faithfully

A. S. Kloss

A. S. Kloss

will

3 Write the responses, using the *will* form of the verb. Use each set of prompts in the box.

afraid/see/till next week ✓	be back from lunch/till 1.30
be back in the office/till Tuesday	invite/bank/manager/lunch
post/tomorrow ✓	put/next bill
send/in two days' time	transfer/money/at the end of the week

e.g. When can we expect the cheque?

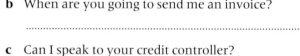

I'll post it tomorrow.

Could you tell your boss to call me.

I'm afraid I won't see her till next week.

a When can I expect payment?

....

b When are you going to send me an invoice?

....

c Can I speak to your credit controller?

....

d You need to ask the bank.

....

e Are you going to invite Rex to Monday's meeting?

....

f You didn't include the delivery charge.

....

Mathematical terms

4 i Write the following in figures and symbols.

e.g. One thousand seven hundred and sixty-five
dollars minus twelve point five per cent.
$$\$1,765 - 12.5\%$$

a Three hundred and twenty-four million divided
by four comes to eighty-one million.

....

b What is fourteen point seven five plus nineteen
point three?

....

c Five thousand, two hundred and one times six.

....

ii Write the following in words.

e.g. $1.7m - 9\frac{1}{4}\%$.
*One point seven million minus
nine and a quarter per cent.*

a $16 + 17.5 - 8 = 25.5$

....

b $£231m \times 16\frac{1}{2}$

....

c $93.2\% \div 4 = 23.3\%$

....

Vocabulary; daily, weekly, etc.

5 Write combinations of these words.

accounts	credit	bank	cheque
control	daily	transfer	book
instalments	card	monthly	statement
deliveries	balance	weekly	payment
terms	totals	account	yearly

e.g. *yearly accounts*   *a bank balance*

....

....

Querying

6 Read the text of a phone call concerning an
incorrect invoice. Correct Sam's notes.

Phone call

M: Hello, Sam. It's Mary Pick here from Glasgow. I'm
calling about your invoice number 29089/1. I notice
that you have invoiced us for four hundred sacks, but
we only ordered three hundred. I've just checked with
our warehouse people, and we have only received three
hundred. We don't need any more.

S: I'm very sorry, Mary. I'll send you another invoice.

M: No, that's not necessary. I could simply subtract the
cost of a hundred sacks from the bill and send you a
cheque for the correct amount.

S: You could, but really I would prefer to send you a new
invoice.

M: OK then. And one other thing. Does the bill include
sales tax?

S: Yes, it does.

M: Oh, it's not clear. Could you make sure it's clearly
stated when you send me the replacement bill?

S: Yes, of course. I'm very sorry about all this.

M: That's OK. Bye.

Mary Pick called about our invoice no.
290981. We invoiced them for 300 sacks,
but they ordered 400. They have
received 300.

Action
Arrange for delivery of 100 more sacks.
Send her a new invoice for 400 sacks.
Make sure that the tax rate is clearly
shown on the invoice.

UNIT 16

Setting up a visit

Some useful phrases

Listen to the recording and repeat

I would (I'd) like to visit the new showroom.

I also need to meet our lawyers.

Could you set up a meeting?

When do you want to come?

What about the week beginning the 10th?

Would week 27 suit you?

> Yes, it would.　No, it would not (wouldn't).

That week is difficult.

It is (It's) a bad time.

Everyone is (Everyone's) busy then. Nobody is (Nobody's) free.

The 29th would be better.

They can only meet you on Tuesday.

See if they are (they're) available at four.

They would (They'd) prefer to meet the following week.

I have (I've) arranged a meeting with Señor Peña for eleven.

I've rescheduled the meeting for 4pm.

I've moved the theatre visit to Wednesday.

Everyone has (Everyone's) confirmed except the group from WZ.

We are (we're) now meeting them at the earlier time of twelve.

That is (That's) 21.00 hours your time.

You are (You're) six hours ahead of us.

He is (He's) going to visit the site first.

Then he's going to have lunch with the staff.

Study notes

Listen to the recording and notice how the final *-th* in ordinal numbers is pronounced:
e.g. *10th, 29th.*

Could you set up a meeting?
Set up is a phrasal verb. We could also say:
Could you arrange a meeting ...?

When do you want to come?
What about the week beginning the 10th?
Revise question words.
See Reference Section 16.1.

Would week 27 suit you?
Revise the use of *would*. Notice how *would* can be used in setting up arrangements.

They would prefer to meet the following week.
Note some other examples of *would/wouldn't*:
Monday would be better.
That wouldn't work.
Would Friday be OK?
See also Reference Section 9.5.

We're now meeting them at the earlier time ...
Note these other examples of the Present Continuous used for plans and arrangements:
She's visiting wholesalers in the afternoon.
So they're coming at 6.30 instead.
Señor Rochas is getting back to me.
See also Reference Section 2.2.

That's 21.00 hours your time.
Note the use of the 24-hour clock in this example. See Reference Section 22.6 for notes on telling the time in English.

Time zones/24-hour clock

1 Listen to people making arrangements in different time zones. Match the times that are equivalent.

a 15.00   i 3.30
b 3.30   ii 8.30
c 12.00   iii 09.00
d 10.30   iv 17.00

Present Continuous for future

2 Write ☐P against the sentences that refer to the present, and ☐F against the sentences that refer to the future.

e.g. I'm going to meet the staff on the 27th.   F
      I'm meeting the staff on the 27th.   F

a It's going to snow.   ☐
  It's snowing.   ☐

b I'm going to learn French.   ☐
  I'm learning French.   ☐

c Are you going to work tomorrow?   ☐
  Are you working tomorrow?   ☐

d He's going to check the figures.   ☐
  He's checking the figures tonight.   ☐

e The company is going to do very well.   ☐
  The company is doing very well.   ☐

f Are you going to meet Mike for lunch?   ☐
  Are you meeting Mike for lunch?   ☐

Arranging a visit

3 Fill in the gaps in the dialogue using words from the box. Practise the dialogue with a partner if possible.

moved	arranged	beginning ✓	see if
possible	suit	available	confirmed
following	difficult		

A: I'd like to visit the new showroom. I also need to meet our lawyers.

B: When do you want to come?

A: What about the week **a** _beginning_ the 10th?

B: That week is **b** .... Everyone is away then. The **c** .... week would be better.

A: I'm afraid that isn't **d** .... for me.

B: Would week 14 **e** .... you?

(*Later.*)

B: I've **f** .... a meeting with Mr Roit for 11.00 on Monday, and I've **g** .... the theatre visit on Wednesday. Everyone has **h** .... except the group from Dacter Ltd.

A: That's good. Thank you. What about the lawyers?

B: They can only meet you at 11.30am on Tuesday. But I could **i** ...., they're **j** .... after lunch the next day.

Question words

4 Write questions to fit the responses.

e.g. – _Why are you coming?_
  – Because I want to meet your agent.

a – How much time ....?
  – About three days.

b – Which day ....?
  – Monday looks free.

c – Who ....?
  – I must see the sales reps. I'd also like to see our distributor and the people from Cordish and Teap.

d – How many days ....?
  – Probably three.

e – Where ....?
  – Could you book me a room at the Casablanca Hotel?

f – When ....?
  – We can have the meeting any time after the 26th.

g – What time ....?
  – See if he can meet me at 2.30pm.

h – How ....?
  – By train.

would

5 Rewrite these sentences using *would*.

e.g. Do you want to meet for a drink?
  Would you like to meet for a drink?

a I want to set up a visit.

....

b Is the 27th possible?

....

c My colleagues prefer the following week.

....

d Are you interested in visiting the new factory?

....

e Can I get you a coffee?

....

f Friday suits me fine.

....

g When do you want to come?

....

h Is it possible to change the time?

....

UNIT 17
Means of travel

Some useful phrases

Listen to the recording and repeat

How do I get to the site?

Where are you coming from?

Visitors usually come by train.

usually	always	often
by train	by plane	by car

The trains are usually on time.

| late | on time | reliable | unreliable |

There are two an hour.

They leave every twenty minutes.

It is (It's) a good service.

How often do you go to Ghent?

About once a month.

| once | twice | three times |

Can you give me directions?

Catch the train to Berlin.

Change in Brussels to the Ghent train.

Get off at Ghent.

Take a taxi to the industrial park.

Is this the right platform for Berlin?

No, you are (you're) on the wrong platform.

You need Platform 1.

I normally go by air in order to save time.

| to save time | to save money |

I sometimes go by train because it saves money.

Study notes

Often can be pronounced /ˈɒftən/ or silent /ˈɒfən/.

How do I get to the site?
We can also say: *How do I reach the site?*

Visitors usually come by train.
Note these common adverbs of frequency:
usually, normally, always, often, sometimes, never.
e.g. *I often travel business class.*   *The trains are usually on time.*
We can't always get a seat.   *Do you sometimes go by bus?*
See also Reference Section 18.4.

About once a month.
Notice these other phrases:
once a day   twice a week   three times a year

Change in Brussels to the Ghent train.
Notice the use of imperatives in giving directions.
Take the train to Ghent.
Ask for the Wetteren Industrial Park.

Is this the right platform for Berlin?
… you're on the wrong platform.
Notice this use of *right* and *wrong*.
Platform = UK English; track = US English.

I normally go by air in order to save time.
I sometimes go by train because it saves money.
These statements answer the question:
Why do you go by air/train?
Note that *in order* can be omitted:
I go by air to save time.
Note also that *because* is followed by *of* when it is used with a noun:
It was because of the cost.
They cancelled the flight because of the weather.

Practice

Travel information

1 Listen to the telephone conversation and complete these notes.

> Train from Paris (Gare de Lyon). Fast train
> (TGV) – a .... an hour. Takes
> b .... Arrives Lyon Petrache.
> Change to the local train to c ....
> Get off in d .... Factory is
> e .... from the station. Take a
> taxi. Ask for f ....

Adverbs frequency

2 Put the adverbs in these sentences.

e.g. (normally) We go by train.

We normally go by train.

a (Usually) The ferry arrives at 10.30.

....

b (often) The train is not late.

....

c (ever) Have you travelled by bullet train?

....

d (once a month) He flies to Tokyo.

....

e (always) Do you travel first class?

....

f (sometimes) I drive to work; it depends on the traffic.

....

g (twice) I have been to Moscow.

....

h (never) There is a taxi when you need one.

....

Getting there

3 Fill in the gaps in the dialogue with suitable words or phrases from the box.

by train	every half hour	get to ✔
get off	how often	reliable
service	take	change

A: How do I _get to_ you?

B: Are you coming from London?

A: Yes, that's right.

B: People from London usually come **a** .... There's a good **b** .... from Waterloo.

A: c .... do the trains leave?

B: There is a train **d** .... , I think. They are very **e** ....

A: How far are you from Southampton?

B: We're about 25 miles from the centre of town. **f** .... at Southampton Central and **g** .... the Portsmouth train. They leave on the hour. **h** .... at Park Gate. We're about three miles from the station.

Why …?, because, (in order) to

4 Match the questions with the answers.

a Why do you go by train? ☐
b Why don't you take the bus? ☐
c Why do you send documents by courier? ☐
d Why do you buy Polish coal? ☐
e Why doesn't your company work flexitime? ☐

i Because it isn't appropriate for our kind of business.
ii To save time.
iii Because I can work during the journey.
iv To save money.
v Because the service isn't reliable enough.

UNIT 18

Travel problems

Some useful phrases

Listen to the recording and repeat

Can you help me?

I have (I've) missed my connection.

I've lost my ticket.

My luggage is missing.

I am (I'm) afraid …

… your visa is not (isn't) valid.

… your passport is out of date.

… the plane is fully booked.

There are no seats available.

There are none at all.

It is (It's) such awful weather that we cannot (can't) take off.

The bad weather started last night.

The fog is so bad that all flights are cancelled.

    fog   gales   floods

The temperature is (temperature's) below zero.

It's over 30 degrees.

It's minus 10.

We regret that …

… the plane is delayed.

… the train is cancelled.

… we have technical problems.

How long is it going to take to sort it out?

It is (It's) difficult to say.

I have no idea.

Soon, I hope.

Study notes

Listen again and notice how these words are said.

booked /bʊkt/   *missed* /mɪst/

delayed /dɪˈleɪd/   *cancelled* /ˈkænsəld/

Compare the pronunciation of started /ˈstɑːtɪd/.

I've missed my connection.

Compare the uses of *miss, lose* and *leave*:

He missed the plane.   He lost his ticket.

He left his briefcase on the train.

There are no seats available.
There are none at all.

Compare the use of *no* and *none*.

See Reference Section 15.2.

It's such awful weather that …
The fog is so bad that …

Note that we use *so* with adjectives and *such* (*a*) with nouns.

See also Reference Section 20.16.

fog, gales, floods

Some other common weather vocabulary:

rain	rainy	rainfall	
sun	sunny	sunshine	
snow	snowy	ice	icy
wind	windy	gales	hurricane
cloud	cloudy	clear	
mist	misty	fog	foggy
storm	thunder	lightning	

The temperature is below zero.

Note that many English-speaking areas, including the US, still give temperatures in Fahrenheit.

Note these other expressions:

over thirty degrees Centigrade

ninety-two degrees Fahrenheit

See also Reference Section 22.10.

Practice

no, none

1 Listen to the recording, make notes and then write sentences using *no* and *none*.

e.g. *The weather was very hot in London last week, but there was no sun at all in Paris.*

a ....

b ....

c ....

d ....

e ....

so, such

2 Write sentences using *so* and *such*.

e.g. (foggy – could drive to work)

It was so foggy that I couldn't drive to work.

a (cold – had to wear a coat)

....

b (much fog – plane could land)

....

c (late – missed train)

....

d (a lot of snow – cancelled the trip)

....

e (bad weather – plane could take off)

....

f (many delays – could make the meeting)

....

g (a wonderful day – went to the beach)

....

h (traffic bad – was an hour late)

....

Visa problems

3 Fill in the gaps in the dialogue using the words and phrases in the box.

depends	difficult	I'm hoping
so	still	the problem
to sort out	valid	where ✓

A: ....*Where*........ are you?

B: I'm sorry I'm **a** .... late. I'm **b** .... at the airport.

A: What's **c** .... ?

B: My visa isn't **d** .... I got it at the Consulate in Madrid, but they say it isn't stamped.

A: Oh no. How long is it going to take **e** .... ?

B: It's **f** .... to say. It **g** .... on the immigration people. **h** .... to catch the train this afternoon.

A: Call us when you have some news.

B: I will.

Weather vocabulary

4 Complete each sentence with a word from the box. There are two more words than you need.

cloudy ✓	flooding	foggy	freezing
hurricane	icy	lightning	raining
snowy	storms	sun	thunder
windy			

e.g. The sky was very _cloudy_ and it was very dark.

a The temperature is below zero and the roads are very ....

b There is a lot of heavy .... and many roads are closed.

c It's very .... – visibility is down to a hundred metres.

d A lot of trees were blown down in the ....

e The .... has destroyed many buildings in the town.

f Our warehouse was hit by .... and caught fire.

g It was .... so hard that we couldn't go out.

h It was very .... and I lost my hat.

i You must wear a coat. It is .... outside.

j The .... is very hot. Make sure you wear a hat.

Travel problems – vocabulary

5 Write examples of travel problems. In each one use a term from Box 1 and a term from Box 2.

Box 1

cancelled ✓	delayed	fully booked	lost
missed	missing	not valid	out of date

Box 2

connecting flight	flight ✓	luggage	passport
plane	ticket	train	visa

e.g. _The flight was cancelled._

a ....

b ....

c ....

d ....

e ....

f ....

g ....

Temperature

6 Write these temperatures in words.

e.g. 27°C _Twenty-seven degrees Centigrade_

a −5°C ....

b 11°C ....

c 75°F ....

d 28°F ....

e −15°C ....

UNIT 19

About the product

Some useful phrases

Listen to the recording and repeat

This is the display room.
We do a wide range of products.
They are available in two sizes.
… and in two colours.

How much does it cost?
Could you tell me how much it costs?
It is (It's) £3,500, excluding VAT.

What does it weigh?
I would (I'd) like to know what it weighs.
It weighs just over 200 kilos.

What size is A5 paper?
It's 210 by 148 millimetres.
What is (What's) the width of the box?
It's 10 centimetres in width.

in width	in length
in height	in depth

It's 10 centimetres wide.

wide	long	high	deep

Could you give us the dimensions?
It's 20 centimetres by 10 by 15.

What is it made of?
It's made of plastic.

wood	glass	fibreglass
rubber	paper	metal

What guarantee do you offer?
It's guaranteed for two years.
It has a one-year warranty.
Is there anything else you would (you'd) like to know?

Study notes

Listen to the recording again and practise the pronunciation of *width* /wɪdθ/, *length* /leŋθ/, *height* /haɪt/ and *depth* /depθ/.

How much does it cost?
What does it weigh?
Compare these examples of direct questions with the indirect questions:
Could you tell me how much it costs?
I'd like to know what it weighs.
See Reference Section 16.2.

What is the width of the box?
It's 10 centimetres in width.
It's 10 centimetres wide.
See also Reference Section 22.9.

Could you give us the dimensions?
Revise the different ways we can describe dimensions:
20 centimetres in length, 10 centimetres in width and 15 centimetres in depth
or 20cm long, 10cm wide, and 15cm deep
or (simply): It's 20cm by 10 by 15.
(The preposition *by* is used here.)

What is it made of?
It's made of plastic.
Do you know these other materials?

tin	*brass*	*lead*	*cardboard*
gold	*concrete*	*zinc*	*silver*

What guarantee do you offer?
Note that *guarantee* can also be used as a verb:
How long is it guaranteed for?

It has a one-year warranty.
It is generally more common for products to have a limited *warranty* than a full *guarantee*.

A product enquiry

1 Listen and correct the memo an IT manager has written after talking to a computer supplier.

> ### Memo
>
> **PRODUCT ENQUIRY: THE ER COMPUTER**
>
> - The ERXJU computer is €2,500 including VAT, so it is within our budget of €5,000 per machine (I didn't ask but I am sure we will get a discount if we buy in quantity).
> - It would fit the space available at most workstations. The base is 25cm × 20cm (weighs 4kg).
> - It comes with a one-year warranty – I need to find in more detail what this covers.

Indirect questions

2 Write direct and indirect questions for these answers.

e.g. – Which colours can we have?

– Could you tell me which colours we can have?

– You can have grey, red or brown.

a – ....

– ....

– It's made of fibreglass.

b – ....

– ....

– I'd like it in blue.

c – ....

– ....

– We'd like to have the large size.

d – ....

– ....

– We need it for photocopying.

e – ....

– ....

– It weighs just over 200 kilos.

Materials

3 i Identify the materials.

a pl _ _ _ _ c   **f** p _ p _ r
b m – t – l   **g** t _ n
c gl _ ss   **h** r _ _ b _ r
d f _ b _ egl _ ss   **i** g _ ld
e w _ _ d   **j** b _ _ ss

ii Indicate what the following are made of.

e.g. (windows) Windows are made of glass.

a (packing cases) ....

b (tyres) ....

c (cans) ....

d (small boats) ....

e (books) ....

f (wedding ring) ....

Weights and measurements

4 Complete the sentences.

e.g. – It's 10 centimetres wide.

– It's 10 centimetres in width.

a – It's 20 metres long.
– It's 20 metres in ....

b – It .... 50kg.
– It's 50kg in weight.

c – How .... is it?
– It's 200m high.
– It's 200m in height.

d – It's 15m deep.
– It's 15m in ....

UNIT 20

About the process

Some useful phrases

Listen to the recording and repeat

Orders are usually received by phone.

by phone	by fax
by post	by email
via our website	

They are keyed into the computer.

Orders are always acknowledged.

Urgent orders are given priority.

Where are the orders processed?

They are processed in this office.

And where are the goods produced?

produced	manufactured	assembled

First, the parts are brought here.

Then they are put into boxes.

After that, the boxes are placed on pallets.

The pallets are lowered.

lowered	raised	wrapped

The finished products are taken to Despatch.

They are loaded onto trucks …

… and they are delivered to the customer.

What happens if an order is delayed?

We contact the customer immediately.

The reason for the delay is explained.

The customer is always kept informed.

We always get back to the customer.

Study notes

Listen to the recording again and practise the pronunciation of the underlined words (-*ed* endings).

And where are the goods <u>produced</u>?
… the boxes are <u>placed</u> on pallets.
The pallets are <u>lowered</u>.
The reason for the delay is <u>explained</u>.
Compare these examples with:
They are <u>loaded</u> onto trucks.

Orders are usually received by phone.
Orders are always acknowledged.

These are examples of the Simple Present Passive. Note the position of *usually* and *always*.
See Reference Sections 5 and 18.1 for further details on the Simple Present Passive and adverbs of frequency.

Where are the orders processed?

Note the question form of the Present Simple Passive. The negative form is:
They are not (aren't) processed here.

First, the parts are bought here.
Then they are put into boxes.
After that, the boxes are placed on pallets.

Note the sequence of events. Some other words which describe a sequence are:

before that	*second*	*next*	*finally*

We always get back to the customer.

Note:
I'll get back to you.
Could you get back to me?
Please keep me informed.

Sequencing

1 Listen to the recording about the production of yoghurt and put the statements in order.

- ☐ The pallets are loaded onto lorries.
- ☐ The pots are sealed.
- ☑ The empty yoghurt pots are brought to the filling line by an automatic conveyor.
- ☐ The pallets are wrapped.
- ☐ The sealed pots are packed in boxes by hand.
- ☐ The boxes are placed on pallets.
- ☐ The pots are filled automatically.
- ☐ The pallets are taken to Despatch.

Comparing Active with Passive Frequency

2 Put the passive sentences into the active.

e.g. Orders are always acknowledged.
   We always acknowledge orders.

a Customers are usually kept informed.

....

b Gifts are sometimes given to customers.

....

c Gifts are never given to suppliers.

....

d Orders are rarely taken on the phone.

....

e Some orders are still sent by fax.

....

Passive forms

3 Complete the sentences with an appropriate verb in the Simple Present or Past Passive.

to ask	to receive	to give	to store ✓
to load	to bring	to take	

e.g. Goods _are stored_ in the warehouse.

a Orders .... via our website.

b Urgent orders .... priority.

c Goods .... to the loading bay by conveyor.

d They .... on to trucks by hand.

e I .... out to dinner yesterday.

f I .... to a very good restaurant.

Instructions

4 Write some instructions on how to make coffee in a coffee machine or cafetière. Use the Simple Present Passive when possible. Note that imperatives can also be used.

e.g. _First fill the kettle with water._
   The machine is switched on. Then
   water is poured into it ... etc.

Some useful language	
coffee machine	filter
jug	lid/top
jar	pour
cup	switch on
boil	tablespoon

UNIT 21

Making comparisons

Some useful phrases

Listen to the recording and repeat

Do you know anything about cameras?
How do they compare?
Can you recommend one?
I would (I'd) recommend this one.

Let me show you these two cameras.
Have you got another one?
We make two other cameras.
Can you show me any others?

This is the best one on the market.
It is (It's) the most reliable.

the quietest	the noisiest
the cheapest	the most expensive

This is the least expensive.

It has the sharpest picture.
It's the most convenient to use.

It is not (isn't) as good as that one.
This one is better.

worse	faster
more reliable	less reliable

This one is cheaper to buy.
It's more expensive to maintain.
It costs more to repair.

Study notes

How do they compare?
You might ask:
Which (one) do you recommend?
Which (one) would you recommend?
You might answer:
I'm afraid I can't recommend that one.
I strongly recommend this one.

Have you got another one?
We make two other cameras.
Can you show me any others?
Note these examples of *another, other* and *others*.
See also Reference Section 15.6.

This is the best one on the market.
It is (it's) the most reliable.
This is the least expensive.
Compare these examples of superlative adjectives with the others in the summary.
See also Reference Section 17.

It is not (isn't) as good as …
We can make comparisons with (*not*) *as … as*.

This one is better.
… more reliable.
… less reliable.
Compare these examples with the other comparative adjectives in the useful phrases.
See also Reference Section 17.

This one is cheaper to buy.
It's more expensive to maintain.
We can also say:
It's the most expensive to maintain.

Comparing brands

1 Listen to the recording and rank the brands of
cheese in terms of their price, taste and packaging
(1 = the best, 3 = the worst).
the best rating   the worst rating

	price	taste	packaging
Brand A	3		
Brand B			
Brand C			

one, other, another, others

2 Complete the gaps with *one, another, other* or *others*.

A: We are having a lot of problems with our
machine workshop in India. Do you know any
a .... good workshops there?

B: Yes, there is b .... in Chennai, and
c .... one just outside the city.

A: Are there any d .... in the country?

B: I don't really know.

A: So, what are the Chennai workshops like?

B: They're OK. At least, the e ....
in central Chennai is. I wouldn't recommend the
f .... one as I don't know much
about it.

Comparing places, etc.

3 Underline the correct answer. Then write examples
of your own.
a Uruguay/Paraguay is the smallest republic in
South America.
b The Caspian Sea (Asia)/Lake Superior (North
America) is the world's largest lake.
c Everest/K2 is the world's highest mountain.
d The Pacific is deeper than/not as deep as the
Atlantic.
e The Nile is longer than/not as long as the Amazon.
f Mexico City/Cairo has the largest population in
the world.

not as … as; less, least

4 Use the notes to write sentences.
e.g. this car – reliable – that car
This car isn't as reliable as that car.
It is less reliable than that one.
It is the least reliable.

a this company – successful – that company

....

....

....

b the watch – expensive – the other watches

....

....

....

c these lenses – durable – those lenses

....

....

....

Comparative and superlative adjectives

5 Complete the table. Give the opposites.

a	tall	*taller*	*the tallest*
	short	....	....
b	economical	....	....
	....	....	....
c	interesting	....	....
	....	....	....
d	rich	....	....
	....	....	....
e	large	....	....
	....	....	....
f	fast	....	....
	....	....	....

UNIT 22

Arranging meetings/appointments

Some useful phrases

Listen to the recording and repeat

What are you doing next week?
Are you free on the 9th of December ?
Can we meet then?
I am (I'm) sorry, but I'm very busy next week.

Can I make an appointment?
Let me check my diary.
I have (I've) got meetings every day except
Tuesday.
Let us (Let's) make it Tuesday then.

How long are you away for?
How long will you be away for?
I'm away … I will (I'll) be away …
… for a week.
… until next Friday.

When will you be back?
I'll be back by Thursday.
I'll be back in two days.

Will you be back by four o'clock?
I should be.
I should be back by then.

What time suits you?
Does three o'clock suit you?
How about three o'clock?
Three o'clock will be fine.

Friday would suit me best.
I'm free on Friday afternoon.

Study notes

What are you doing next week?
Revise the use of the Present Continuous for future plans:
I'm meeting Ron on Wednesday.   We're having lunch together.
See Reference Section 3.2.

How long are you away for?
How long will you be away for?
I'm away …
I'll be away …
In these examples, either the Simple Present or *will* can be used.
See Reference Section 3 for further details.

… for a week.
… until next Friday.
Note these other examples of *for* and *until*:
I'm/I'll be away for two days/months.
I'm/I'll be away until the end of the week.
See Reference Section 20.12.
Note also:
I'll be back <u>by</u> Thursday   I'll be back <u>in</u> two days.

Will you be back by four o'clock?
I should be.
This is an example of *should* for prediction. The speaker expects to be back by four o'clock.
See also Reference Section 9.4.

Friday would suit me best.
Note the use of *to suit*:
It suits me.
(not *It suits to me* **or** *It suits for me*.)

… on Friday afternoon.
Note when *on* is used:
on Tuesday, on Monday morning, etc.
See Reference Section 19.1 for prepositions of time.

Practice

Taking messages

1 Listen to the recordings and take down the messages.

a
Linda called. She can't make Friday's meeting ...

b

c

d

should *in predictions/*
Present Simple for the future

2 Respond to the statements. Use *should*, *will* or the Present Simple in your answers.

e.g. – Will you be back by four o'clock?
   – I *should be* (be). My meeting ends at 3.30.

a – How long are you away for?
   – I'm not sure. I .... (be) back by Friday.
b – When does your flight leave?
   – It .... (leave) in half an hour. I must hurry.
c – What time do we arrive at LAX Airport?
   – I think we .... (arrive) at ten o'clock.
d – When do you think they will get our letter?
   – They .... (get) it tomorrow, but the post is very unreliable.

e – Could you let me know the arrangements?
   – Of course. I .... (call) you in ten minutes.
f – Do you know when the delivery is due to arrive?
   – It .... (arrive) tomorrow; I hope there are no problems at customs.
g – How long are you here for?
   – I .... (leave) on Sunday.
h – Are you free tomorrow?
   – I .... (have) a meeting in the morning but it .... (finish) at 11.30.

Prepositions of time

3 Complete the sentences using *by, until/till, in* or *for*.

e.g. I'll be out of the office *until/till* Wednesday.

a When will you be back? Will you be back .... Friday?
b I should be back .... the weekend.
c I'll be away .... two days.
d I'll be back .... two weeks' time.
e Are you away .... Monday?
f No, I'm away .... the end of the week.
g We should be back in the office .... 3pm.
h I'll be in the office .... the rest of the week.

Emailing arrangements

4 Write brief replies to the emails as follows.

Message A – accept
Message B – reject
Message C – suggest alternative arrangements

A

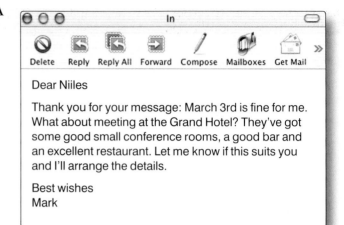

Dear Niiles

Thank you for your message: March 3rd is fine for me. What about meeting at the Grand Hotel? They've got some good small conference rooms, a good bar and an excellent restaurant. Let me know if this suits you and I'll arrange the details.

Best wishes
Mark

B

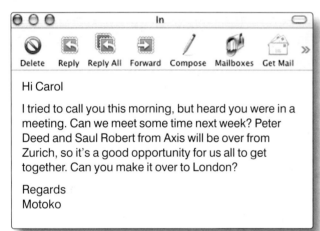

Hi Carol

I tried to call you this morning, but heard you were in a meeting. Can we meet some time next week? Peter Deed and Saul Robert from Axis will be over from Zurich, so it's a good opportunity for us all to get together. Can you make it over to London?

Regards
Motoko

C

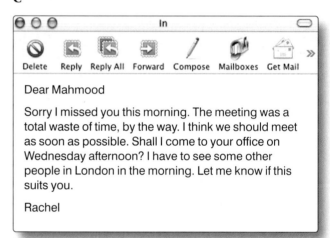

Dear Mahmood

Sorry I missed you this morning. The meeting was a total waste of time, by the way. I think we should meet as soon as possible. Shall I come to your office on Wednesday afternoon? I have to see some other people in London in the morning. Let me know if this suits you.

Rachel

Calling about meeting

5 Put the dialogue in the correct order.

- ☐ It's Roland Pasquale.
- ☐ Good morning. Can I speak to Lucy Stubbs?
- ☑ Stubbs Engineering. Good morning.
- ☐ Do you know when she'll be back?
- ☐ She should be back at five o'clock.
- ☐ Can I leave a message?

- ☐ Could you tell her that Roland Pasquale called about Tuesday's meeting? Thank you.
- ☐ Who's calling?
- ☐ Yes, of course.
- ☐ One moment, please. … I'm afraid there's no answer.

UNIT 23

Checking programmes and schedules

Some useful phrases

Listen to the recording and repeat

Can I check the details?

I need to check some details.

Have I got it right?

Am I right in thinking …

… that you are (you're) arriving on Friday?

… that you are (you're) going to be late?

The form is not (isn't) very clear.

It says that you are (you're) arriving on Saturday.

It says here your name is Becket
– spelt B-E-C-K-E-T.

Is that right?

Yes, that's right.

Can I check when the programme starts?

Can I check that it starts at 2.15?

Yes, it does.

Could you run through the programme?

I will (I'll) run through the programme for you

We need 4,000 units by the end of the week.

Are you sure that you can deliver by then?

Will there be anyone to receive the goods?

I'm afraid no one works on Saturdays.

What is (What's) the delivery schedule?

Could you let us know?

We can let you have 2,000 boxes immediately …

… and the balance of the order by Friday.

Study notes

Have I got it right?

Note these questions:

Have you got that?   *Did you get that?*   *Is that clear?*

Am I right in thinking that you are arriving on Friday?

Can I check when the programme starts?

Can I check that it starts at 2.15?

We often use indirect questions when checking information. See Reference Section 16.2.

Yes, that's right.

Some other responses:

Yes, I've got that [it].   *Everything's* [it's] *clear.*

Sorry, could you say that [it] *again.*

It says that you're arriving on …

It says here your name is …

We can use *It says* when checking information on a form.

Will there be anyone to receive the goods?

I'm afraid no one works on Saturdays.

Note the use of *anyone* and *no one*.

Compare this with:

Surely someone works on Saturdays.

See Reference Section 15.1.

Could you let us know?

We can let you have 2,000 boxes immediately …

Note these other phrases with *let*:

Could you let me know next week?

I'll let you know tomorrow.

See Reference Section 20.1.

Running through an itinerary

1 Listen and fill in the gaps in the programme.

SAT **a** ....
Arrive New York
Hotel –   Bright's Hotel, 5th Avenue and 55th Street.
           Tel. 289760/734500.

MON JAN 18
b ....   Meeting in our offices with Ben West and Ted Luce of
                    Bison Inc.
pm   Open so far.

TUES JAN 19
8.00am   A car will pick you up from **c** .... and
            drive you to meet Barbara Port at 10am.
3.30pm   A car will take you to Laguardia Airport for flight to
            Toronto (leaves **d** .... arrives 7.05pm
            American Airlines 912).
Hotel in Toronto – **e** .... , 59 Avenue Road.

WED JAN 20
am   Meeting with **f** .... (will confirm
            names and time later).
pm   Free.

---

no one, someone, anyone, *etc.*

2 Complete the gaps with *somewhere/anywhere/
nowhere*, *something/anything/nothing* or
someone/anyone/no one. In some cases, there is more
than one possibility.

a I don't know .... to go in this town.

b There is .... to see in this town.

c There is .... to go.

d I know .... we could go to.

e I know .... who could help you.

f I know .... about opera.

g .... sent me an application form.

let

3 Rewrite the sentences using *let*.

e.g. I'll post it on the way home.
Let me post it on the way home.

Really, you mustn't pay!
Really, I can't let you pay.

a It'll be OK – I'll speak to their MD.
....

b Did you give permission for everyone to go
home early?
....

c I prevented them from seeing the plans.
....

d Can you deliver on Thursday?
....

e Could you inform me what happens?
....

Some telephone vocabulary

4 Revise some telephone vocabulary.
e.g. I needed to c.*all*. a client.

a I didn't know his telephone n............................ .

b I looked it up in the d............................ .

c I phoned directory e............................ .

d But his number was not l............................ .

e I called earlier but you were e............................ .

f Your line was b............................ all morning.

g You are always o............................ the phone.

h I got t............................ in the end.

i But it was a terrible l............................ .

j I tried to s............................ to you this morning.

k I also sent you a t..................... message.

UNIT 24

A change of plans

Some useful phrases

Listen to the recording and repeat

I am (I'm) sorry I cannot (can't) make Thursday's meeting.

Can we meet tomorrow instead?

Yes, of course.

That is (That's) not a problem.

Shall we meet on Friday instead?

Why do we not (don't we) make it Friday?

Let's meet on Friday.

That suits me.

Good idea.

I'm afraid that does not (doesn't) suit me.

Can we change the date?

    the date   the time   the place

No problem.

Yuri can't come on Tuesday.

He is (He's) too busy.

He has (He's) broken his arm.

I'm sorry to hear that.

Please pass on my best wishes.

Can we make it just after 4.00?

    just before 3.15

    not later than three o'clock

    at about 5.30

    at around 5.45

We can not (can't) hold the meeting in the hotel.
There was a fire there last night.

    a flood   an explosion

    a bomb warning   a power cut

Study notes

Listen again and compare the final /iːn/ sound in *3.15* with the final /ɪ/ sound in *5.30*.

Can we meet tomorrow instead?
We can also say:
Can we meet tomorrow instead of next week?

Yes, of course.
That's no problem.
That suits me.
No problem.
Notice these responses to a suggested change of plans.

Shall we meet on Friday instead?
Shall is only used with *I* or *we* for suggestions.
Let's meet is less formal than *shall we meet*.
See Reference Section 20.4.

Why don't we make it Friday?
Why don't …? is often used with *we* but can be used with all persons:
Why don't I call you later?
Why don't you change the date?
See Reference Section 20.4.

just after 4.00
just before 3.15
not later that three o'clock
at about 5.30
at around 5.45
Note these examples of approximate time.
Compare:
at four o'clock
at 5.30 sharp

We can't hold the meeting …
Instead of *hold* we can say *have* the meeting.

Reasons for not attending

1 Listen to the recordings. What is the problem?

e.g. ....He's broken his leg.....

a ....

b ....

c ....

d ....

e ....

Why don't we ...?

2 Re-write the sentences with *Why don't/doesn't ...?*

e.g. Shall we change the date?
.....Why don't we change the date?.....

a Can't she put the meeting off till next week?
....

b Could we make it just after three o'clock?
....

c Shall I meet you in a hotel?
....

d Shall we meet on Friday instead?
....

e Let's send her a 'get well' card.
....

f Would you like to take the day off?
....

Expressions of time

3 Put the following in order, where 1 is definitely the earliest appointment, and 8 is the latest.

a I'll see you at about half past three. ☐

b I'll see you at three-forty sharp. ☐

c Why don't we make it a little after a quarter to four? ☐

d Shall we put it off until a quarter to four? ☐

e Can we make it no later than ten past five? ☐

f Can we make it just after five o'clock? ☐

g Let's make it nearer to four-thirty. ☐

h Can we leave it until just after twenty past three? ☐ 1

Approximate times

4 Read the dialogue and tick [✓] the times that fit with what the speaker says.

A: Woman   **B:** Man

A: When did they call you?

B: I can't remember exactly. It was certainly early in the morning. Just before seven, I think. I heard the clock strike seven after they rang.

A: So when did you leave the hotel?

B: At around 7.30. No, it was later than 7.30, because I listened to the 7.30 news before I left.

A: And what time did you get to the office?

B: At about eight. We started the meeting at 8.15, just after Pat arrived. It was nearly twelve when we finished.

a The people called at   6.50 ✓ 6.58 ✓ 7.00 ☐

b He left the hotel at   7.28 ☐ 7.37 ☐ 7.31 ☐

c He reached the office at   7.55 ☐ 8.05 ☐ 8.10 ☐

d Pat arrived at   7.50 ☐ 8.10 ☐ 8.15 ☐

e The meeting finished at   11.55 ☐ 12.00 ☐ 12.10 ☐

UNIT 25
Eating out

Listen to the recording and repeat

Would you like to go out for a meal tonight?

Thank you. I would (I'd) like that very much.

Do you have a reservation?

We have a reservation for eight o'clock.

The name is Moeller.

This way, please.

Are you ready to order?

What will you have to start with?

What would you like for the main course?

What vegetables would you like?

It comes with rice or potatoes.

I will not (won't) have either.

Can I have both?

I will (I'll) have a salad.

What sort of salad would you like?

    sort of   type of   kind of

What kind of steak would you like?

How do you like your steak?

Rare. Medium. Well done.

Would you like something to drink?

Would you like anything else?

We would like (we'd like) a bottle of water.

    a glass of wine.   a cup of coffee.

    a piece of cheese.   a box of chocolates.

Could we see the dessert menu?

And can we have the bill, please?

Study notes

Listen again. Notice that in expressions like *a cup of coffee*, often *of* is pronounced /əv/.

Do you have a reservation?

Notice these other common expressions:

Do you have a booking?   *Have you reserved a table?*
Have you booked a table?   *We have a table booked for …*

It comes with … potatoes.

Note also:

How does it come?
What does it come with?

I won't have either.
Can I have both?

Revise *either/or* and *both/and*:

The dish comes with (either) rice or potatoes.
The service was (both) quick and friendly.

Note that here *either/both* can be omitted.

See Reference Section 15.5.

I'll have a salad.

Notice how *will* can be used in ordering a meal.

See Reference Section 3.4 to revise the use of *will*.

What sort of salad would you like?

Note that *kind of* and *type of* can also be used.

How would you like your steak?
Rare. Medium. Well done.

Steak can also be served *medium rare* and even *very well done*!

… a bottle of water.

Revise these expressions.

a packet of rice	*a can of beer*	*a glass of milk*
a cup of coffee	*a pot of coffee*	*a piece of cheese*
a plate of sandwiches	*a bowl of fruit*	*a jug of water*
a list of restaurants	*a pot of tea*	*a loaf of bread*

Practice

Reserving a table

1 Listen to the dialogues and fill in the booking list.

Tuesday 17th February			
Name	Day	Time	Number
Lever	....	....	....
....	....	....	....
....	....	....	....

Food vocabulary

2 Match the words in the box with the vocabulary groups.

vegetables	starters	meat
desserts	kinds of salad	flavours of ice-cream
cold drinks	coffees	types of fruit juice
steaks ✓	fish	

e.g. rare, medium, well done .... *steaks* ....

a soup, paté, prawn cocktail ....

b lager, mineral water, milkshake ....

c green, tomato, mixed ....

d chicken, pork, veal ....

e trout, salmon, plaice ....

f black, white, with sugar ....

g chocolate pudding, fruit salad, apple pie ....

h orange, tomato, grapefruit ....

i vanilla, chocolate, strawberry ....

j peas, carrots, broccoli ....

a bottle, a cup, *etc.*

3 **i** Complete the phrases with expressions from the box.

e.g. .... *a pot of* .... coffee

a bottle of	a box of	a cup of	a glass of	a list of
a piece of	a pot of ✓	a range of	a selection of	a slice of

a .... chocolate cake
b .... fruit
c .... tea
d .... matches
e .... mineral water
f .... toast
g .... services

ii Write short exchanges using the phrases.

e.g. – Could we have a pot of coffee for two, please?

  – Certainly.

either … or, both … and

4 Fill in the gaps using *both* or *either*.

a – If you're having the set menu, you can have .... *either* .... soup or paté.

  – Then I'll have soup.

b – The fish comes with rice or noodles.

  – I won't have .... , thank you. I'll just have a side salad.

c – Would you like French dressing or blue cheese dressing with your salad?

  – I don't know. They're .... delicious.

  – I can recommend the blue cheese.

d – Do you want your fish grilled or fried?

  – Which do you recommend?

  – They are .... very good.

e – If I have a set menu, do I get avocado with prawns or avocado with vinaigrette?

  – You can have .... Which would you prefer?

UNIT 26
Leisure activities

Some useful phrases

Listen to the recording and repeat

Do you play squash?

    squash   golf   tennis

Would you like a game?

Do you like swimming?

Would you like to go for a swim?

    swim   run   walk

I enjoy watching TV very much.

So do I.

I am (I'm) not very keen on running.

Neither am I.

I cannot (can't) stand golf.

I can't stand it either.

I prefer tennis.

I do too.

Do you like going to the ballet?

    the ballet   the opera

    the theatre   the cinema

I used to go to the cinema a lot.

Let us (Let's) get some tickets.

I used to play squash a lot too.

Why do not (don't) we have a game?

Will you have any free time while you are (you're) here?

Can you get away?

Could you take some time off?

Study notes

Do you play squash?
Note these other questions:

Why don't we go for a ride some time?   *Do you play [golf]?*
Would you like a game of [tennis]?   *Where do you play?*

Note these noun/verb forms:

Verb:		**Noun:**	
	to walk		*a walk*
	to run		*a run*
	to sail		*a sail*
	to ride		*a ride*
	to swim		*a swim*

Do you like swimming?
Note that *like, love, hate, prefer* are usually followed by the verb in the *-ing* form in UK English:
I like walking.
In US English, they are usually followed by the infinitive:
I like to walk.
See Reference Section 8.

I enjoy watching TV very much.
Note that *enjoy, be keen on, cannot stand* are followed by the verb in the *-ing* form:
I enjoy playing golf.

So do I.
Neither am I.
Note that *so* and *too* are used in the affirmative:
– *I'm very keen on ballet.*   – *So am I. / I am too.*
In the negative, we use *neither/nor* and *either*:
– *I can't stand running.*   – *Neither/Nor can I. / I can't either.*

I used to go to the cinema a lot.
Used to is used for regular actions or events in the past that no longer happen:
I used to play tennis twice a week, but now I only play once a month.
I used to work in the Milan office.
See also Reference Section 20.9.

Practice

Confirming an arrangement

1 i Listen to the two dialogues. Which one relates to the email below?

ii Write an email in which you confirm the arrangements suggested in the other dialogue.

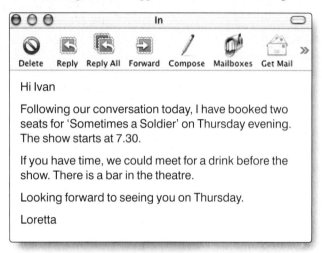

Hi Ivan

Following our conversation today, I have booked two seats for 'Sometimes a Soldier' on Thursday evening. The show starts at 7.30.

If you have time, we could meet for a drink before the show. There is a bar in the theatre.

Looking forward to seeing you on Thursday.

Loretta

so, neither (nor), too, either

2 Respond to the sentences with *so/neither* (*nor*) or *too/either*.

e.g. I enjoy walking very much.
  .....*So do I* **or** ...*I do too.*...

  I'm not very keen on running.
  .....*Neither am I* **or** ...*I'm not either.*

a I could take some time off this afternoon.

....

b I don't like going to the opera.

....

c I used to like the opera very much.

....

d I'll have some free time tomorrow.

....

e I can't stand watching athletics.

....

f I used to play squash once or twice a week.

....

used to

3 Complete these examples using *used to*.

e.g. ...*We used to have an office in Milan*..., but it closed three years ago.

a ...., but now we employ fewer than 1,000.

b .... Now we import them from Singapore.

c .... Now we open at 8.30.

d ...., but we moved it to Shanghai last year.

e ...., but now I don't play at all.

f ...., but now I don't enjoy them.

g .... Now I don't have time.

h .... Now I have a job with SRT.

Games and pastimes

4 Make vocabulary sets.

e.g. tennis — sailing — American football

a swimming — wrestling — opera
b football — classical — judo
c ballet — magazines — bridge
d boxing — squash — newspapers
e chess — theatre — folk
f jazz — rugby — badminton
g detective novels — draughts — windsurfing

UNIT 27
Nightlife

Some useful phrases

Listen to the recording and repeat

What are we going to do?

Where shall we go?

Shall we go to a club?

I must go back to the hotel.

I must go to bed.

I have to get up early tomorrow.

I have to catch a plane.

Is it possible to get a meal round here?

Where can we get a drink?

Does anyone want to go for a coffee?

I know a place in Main Street.

How much does it cost to get in?

Are you a member?

They are (They're) my guests.

They're friends of mine.

It is (It's) my round.

Can we have another bottle?

Do you serve food?

Can we have …

… a few more sandwiches?

… a little more coffee?

Can you put the drinks on my bill, please?

Could we have our bill, please?

Study notes

Where shall we go?
Shall we go to a club?
Note the use of *shall* in making suggestions and asking for suggestions.
See also Reference Section 20.4.

I must go back to the hotel.
I have to catch a plane.
Compare the use of *must* and *have to*.
Both express obligation or necessity, and often either can be used:
I have to call the office.   *We have to pay that bill.*
or *I must call the office.*   **or** *We must pay that bill.*
In the negative, the meanings are different:
You mustn't go to work. (You're ill.)
You don't have to go to work. (It's a public holiday.)
See Reference Section 9.3 for further details.

Where can we get a drink?
Can we have another bottle?
Could we have our bill, please?
See Reference Section 9.1 for notes on *can/could*.

They're friends of mine.
Note that we cannot say *friends of me*.
Notice that nouns and names can also be used:
a customer of Bob's
a friend of the managing director's
See Reference Section 13.2 for possessive pronouns (*mine, yours*).

a few more sandwiches
a little more coffee
Revise the use of *a few* and *a little*. Note that they both mean *some*.
A few is used with plural nouns: *a few drinks, a few friends.*
A little is used with uncountable nouns:
a little time, a little money.
See also Reference Section 15.4.

Practice

A thank you letter

1 Listen to the recording. Which dialogue relates to the thank you letter below? Write a thank you email for the other dialogue.

> Dear Aida
>
> I would like to thank you for a wonderful evening. I enjoyed the Fado Club we went to very much. It was a great pleasure to hear traditional Portuguese music.
>
> I look forward to returning your hospitality when you visit the UK next. If you come after September, we can go to a Liverpool match.
>
> Please give my regards to Charles.
>
> With best wishes.
>
> Harvey

must, have to

2 Complete the sentences using *must, mustn't, have to, don't have to* or *had to*.

e.g. I feel very tired. I *must/have to* get some sleep.

a He .... wear a suit at work. It's company policy.
b What a good idea. We .... do that.
c You .... forget to call Derek before twelve.
d She .... go to Spain three times last year.
e We all .... pay taxes. It's the law.
f We .... close down the factory. It was losing money.
g Everybody in the company .... start work at 8am.
h I .... oversleep tomorrow. I've got an important meeting at 7.45.
i It's good that I .... get up early tomorrow.

a friend of mine, *etc.*

3 Complete the phrases.

e.g. one of my friends
= *a friend of mine*
some of our products
= some products of ours

a one of Mr Fenn's colleagues
= ....
b some of their customers
= ....
c ....
= a proposal of yours
d one of Tim's suggestions
= ....
e ....
= an advertisement of ours
f some of his ideas
= ....

a few, a little

4 Complete the examples using *a few* or *a little*.

e.g. – Have you got any dollars left?
– I've got *a few* .

a – Can we have .... more sandwiches?
b – It took us .... days to reach Moscow.
c – Have you got any money?
– I have ....
d – Can we have .... more coffee?
e – We have .... time left before your flight leaves.
f – Who knows about this?
– .... people know about it, but not many.
g – We haven't got enough petrol.
– There's .... in the spare can.

UNIT 28
The market

Some useful phrases

Listen to the recording and repeat

Where are your main markets?
The Caribbean region is our biggest market.
The US is also a good market for us.

There is (There's) a good market for our products in Central America.

... the Middle East.   ... West Africa.
... Australasia.   ... South-East Asia.
... Eastern Europe.   ... Central Asia.

The total market is worth £50 million a year.
The market has grown quickly.
The market is now growing more slowly.

How are things going in South America?
We are doing very well there.
There is (There's) a growing demand for our products.
We have increased our market share by 10%.

We are doing even better in North America.
We are working harder than our competitors.
We are operating more effectively than our competitors.

We export leather bags.
... high-quality leather bags.
... high-quality Italian leather bags.
China is an exciting new market for us.

We imported $54 million worth of goods last year.
We provided services worth $1.2 billion.
We sold $2 million worth of equipment.

Study notes

Notice that *10%* is pronounced *ten per cent* (not *ten pro cent*).

There's a good market for our products in the Middle East.
Some other regions:

North America	*East Africa*	*Central America*
Western Europe	*South America*	*Northern Europe*
North Africa	*Southern Europe*	*Southern Africa*
The Far East	*Asia Pacific*	*Oceania*

The market is now growing more slowly.
Note these other examples of comparative adverbs.
We are doing better in North America.
We are working harder ...
We are operating more effectively ...
See Reference Section 18.8.

How are things going in South America?
Note these other questions:
How's business going in ...?
How's it going in ...?

We export high-quality Italian leather bags.
Notice the order of these adjectives.
See Reference Section 17.1 for guidelines.

China is an exciting new market for us.
You can also say:
The market is new and exciting.
or *It's a new and exciting market.*
or *It's a new exciting market.*
(But not *The market is new, exciting.*)

We sold $2 million worth of equipment.
When spoken, this is:
... two million dollars worth of ...
See Reference Section 22.1 for more on high numbers.

Main markets

1 Match the speakers with the markets.

'Where are your main markets?'

a	An agrochemicals consultant	**i**	The Middle East
b	A PR manager	**ii**	East European markets
c	A senior administrative manager	**iii**	South-East Asia
d	A marketing director	**iv**	Asia-Pacific
e	A sales executive	**v**	The US market

The order of adjectives

2 Put the adjectives into an appropriate order.

e.g. a(n)/Japanese/interesting/new/design

an interesting new Japanese design

a a/new/beautiful/Jaguar

....

b a(n)/Spanish/manager/experienced

....

c a/wooden/table/large

....

d a/new/challenge/market

....

e a(n)/ugly/building/red

....

f the/training/old/department

....

g a(n)/briefcase/leather/expensive/Italian

....

h a(n)Swiss/company/medium-sized/manufacturing

....

Comparative adverbs

3 Complete the sentences with a comparative adverb.

e.g. Things are moving very slowly.

They need to move ...*more quickly*... .

a We have arranged things badly in the past. We need to arrange things .... in the future.

b Our agent worked very inefficiently last year. He must work .... this year.

c His monthly reports were always late. They always arrived .... than the others.

d He says he works hard. He say he works .... than anyone else.

e He doesn't work intelligently. He works .... than his colleagues.

f Round here, things don't change very fast. But I'll think they'll change .... in future.

g I'm afraid I don't understand when you speak quickly. Could you speak a little .... , please.

h The problem is that we're not marketing aggressively enough. To succeed in a competitive area like this, we have to market ....

Numbers

4 Write these numbers in words.

a 103 ....

b 145 ....

c 45th ....

d 27,987 ....

e 456,901 ....

f 3,001,908 ....

g 65bn ....

h 23rd ....

UNIT 29

Distribution

Some useful phrases

Listen to the recording and repeat

Do you have your own lorries?

> trucks   trailers
> containers   railway wagons

Do you own them or do you lease them?
We lease them.

We do not (don't) have our own transport department.
We subcontract to a local haulage company.
We use a local haulier.
We have (We've) outsourced our logistics.

I have (I've) been trying to contact you all morning.
What have you been doing?
I've been doing some paperwork.
I've been organising a delivery.

I am (I'm) calling about a delivery.
We still have not (haven't) received it.
Do you know what has happened to it?
I'll check for you.

We have (We've) been having …
We've had …
… a lot of problems recently.

Deliveries have been arriving …
… late.   … damaged.
Orders have been short.

Things have been going badly.

Study notes

Do you have your own lorries?
Own can be used as an adjective.

trucks/trailers
Note these terms:
road transport   *rail freight*   *air freight*

Do you own them …?
Own can also be used as a verb – but not in the Present Continuous. (We cannot say *Are you owning them?*)
Note also *to have*:
We have our own fleet of lorries. (Not *We are having our own fleet of lorries.*)
See Reference Section 2.4.

We lease them.
Note also *to rent* and *to hire*:
I often hire a car.   *We are renting the equipment.*

We have outsourced our logistics.
to outsource = to subcontract
logistics = the planning and control of the flow of goods

I've been trying to contact you all morning.
What have you been doing?
Note these examples of the Present Perfect Continuous.
See Reference Section 2.9.

We still haven't received it.
Do you know what has happened to it?
Notes these examples of the Simple Present Perfect.
See Reference Section 2.8.

We've been having a lot of problems recently.
We've had a lot of problems …
In these examples, either the Present Perfect Continuous or the Present Perfect Simple can be used.

Practice

A late delivery

1 Listen to the dialogue and complete the statements below.

e.g. Donya Reed works ....for AR Chemicals.......

a Mr Martin has been trying ....

b He wants to know where Ms Reed ....

c Ms Reed has just ....

d She doesn't know where her colleagues are because ....

e Mr Martin is calling because ....

f He spent all day yesterday ....

g And .... all morning.

h Ms Reed promises to ....

Vocabulary

2 Complete the sentences with words from the box.

fleet	vans ✓	distribution network
forwarding	warehouses	air freight
rail freight	subcontract	

e.g. We use small ....vans........ for local deliveries.

a We .... most of our transport business to a national haulage company.

b They have an excellent .... which covers the whole country.

c They have their own .... of lorries.

d They have excellent contacts with .... agents in the major ports.

e Their .... are located near our major customers.

f They use .... when they want to move goods quickly.

g They normally use .... when deliveries are not so urgent.

Present Perfect Continuous

3 Write answers to the question: *You look tired. What have you been doing?*

e.g. (send/emails)
...I've been sending emails all morning.......

a (make/phone calls)
....

b (play/tennis)
....

c (argue/with the accounts department)
....

d (move/boxes all morning)
....

e (have/lunch with some customers)
....

f (work/on some sales figures)
....

g (nothing, but I/not/sleep/well)
....

Contrasting Present Perfect Simple, Present Perfect Continuous and Simple Past

4 Make sentences using the Present Perfect Simple, the Present Perfect Continuous or the Simple Past.

e.g. I – send – a customer an express parcel yesterday.

I sent a customer an express parcel yesterday.

a He – call – this morning.

....

b He – not – receive – it yet.

....

c I – try – contact the courier since then.

....

d He – not – answer his phone.

....

e We – have – a lot of problems with our courier service recently.

....

f Deliveries – arrive late.

....

g Deliveries – get lost.

....

h I – decide to end their contract.

....

Contrasting Present Perfect Simple and Present Perfect Continuous

5 Tick the sentences which are possible.

e.g. We've waited two weeks for the delivery. ☑
We've been waiting two weeks for the delivery. ☑

a I've left my car at home today. ☐
I've been leaving my car at home today. ☐

b We've been using Framptons quite a lot recently. ☐
We've used Framptons a lot recently. ☐

c I've finished all the paperwork. ☐
I've been finishing the paperwork. ☐

d We've received three of the four parcels. ☐
We've been receiving three of the four parcels. ☐

e Have we been hearing from the subcontractors? ☐
Have we heard from the subcontractors? ☐

Verbs of possession

6 Answer the questions for your own company or for a company you know. Then write a brief statement summarising your answers.

a Do you have your own lorries/vans?
b If so, do you own them or do you lease them?
c Do you have your own transport department?
d Do you use to a specialist courier company?
e If so, do you use a local courier or a national company?

e.g. _We don't have our own lorries. We subcontract all our deliveries_ ... etc.

UNIT 30

The competition

Some useful phrases

Listen to the recording and repeat

Who are your main competitors?
They are Alpha, Beta and Gamma.
How do they compare in terms of size?
Which company is the market leader?

Beta is a subsidiary of Remo.
It has excellent local representation.
Its headquarters are in Houston.
Its prices are very competitive.

Alpha is slightly smaller than Beta.
It is (It's) a slightly smaller company.
Its prices are a little lower.
Its overheads are slightly higher.

Gamma is much bigger than Beta.
It's a much bigger company.
Its prices are a lot higher.
Its overheads are much higher.
They are far higher.

In terms of size, Gamma is by far the biggest company.
They are by far the most successful.
They are far more successful than Beta.

It's a good company.
They are (They're) a good company.
The group works well together.
The group work well together.

The news is good.
The information is clear.

Study notes

Its headquarters are in Houston.
Headquarters takes a singular or plural verb: *Our headquarters is/are in Houston.*
Head office takes a singular verb: *Our head office is in Seoul.*

Alpha is slightly smaller than Beta.
It's a slightly smaller company.
Its prices are a little lower.
Its overheads are slightly higher.
Not these examples of *slightly* and *a little* with comparative adjectives.
Note the contraction of *it is* to *it's*.
Compare these examples:
It's a slightly smaller company.   Its prices are a little lower.

Gamma is much bigger than Beta.
It's a much bigger company.
It's prices are a lot higher.
They are far higher.
Note these examples of *much*, *a lot* and *far*. *Far* can replace *much* or *a lot*.
See Reference Section 17.4.

In terms of size …
We could also say: *in terms of quality, in terms of market share,* etc.

… Gamma is by far the biggest company.
Note the use of *by far* with superlative adjectives.

It's a good company.
They're a good company.
The group works/work well together.
Some other common nouns which take a singular or plural verb:
team   family   group   committee

The news is good.
These nouns also take a singular verb:
equipment   furniture   information   advice
See Reference Section 12.2.

Practice

Talking about the competition

1 Listen to the recording and note down the main point each speaker makes.

'How do you compare with the competition?'

a Speaker 1

   Our products are much cheaper.

b Speaker 2

   ....

c Speaker 3

   ....

d Speaker 4

   ....

e Speaker 5

   ....

Vocabulary extension

2 Complete the table. Mark the word stress by underlining it.

comp<u>e</u>titor	comp<u>e</u>tition	to comp<u>e</u>te
producer	....	....
employer	....	....
supplier	....	....
distributor	....	....
manufacturer	....	....
manager	....	....
administrator	....	....
organiser	....	....

Nouns followed by a singular or plural verb

3 Complete the sentences with *is* or *are*. Both are possible in some cases.

e.g. Our company headquarters ....*is/are*......... in Moscow.

a The outskirts of town .... not very beautiful.

b One of our directors .... coming next week.

c The company .... very profitable.

d We .... a well-managed company.

e The company's reputation .... good.

f What .... the latest news?

g The new equipment .... arriving tomorrow.

h The new range of products .... excellent.

i .... your group meeting tomorrow?

Degrees of size

4 i Put the following phrases in order of size where 1 is the biggest and 8 is the smallest.

ii Write examples comparing the firms in your field, using as many of the phrases as possible.

a lot bigger ☐   far bigger ☐

much bigger ☐   not much bigger ☐

slightly bigger ☐   marginally bigger ☐

very much bigger ☐   by far the biggest ☐

UNIT 31

Forecasting

Some useful phrases

Listen to the recording and repeat

Do you expect sales to rise next month?
I think they are (they're) likely to fall.
They're unlikely to increase.
Sales are certain to fall.
It is (It's) difficult to forecast.

We have (We've) budgeted for a 5% increase.
We will (We'll) continue to expand …
… in the short term.
… in the medium term.
… in the long term.
… during the summer.

We expect the figure will be down …
… in the first quarter of the year.
… in the second quarter.
… in the third quarter.
… in the final quarter.

We are expecting sales …
… to fall back during the autumn.
… to remain stable in the winter.
… to pick up in the spring.

If the dollar falls in value, we will sell more abroad.
We'll be able to export more if the dollar falls.
We'll make more profit if we can reduce costs.

Study notes

Notice the word stress in phrases like *in the short term* and *in the medium term*, *in the first quarter* and *in the second quarter*. Listen and practise.

I think they're likely to fall.
They're unlikely to increase.
Sales are certain to fall.

Notice how we use *likely*, *unlikely* and *certain* to express different degrees of certainty.

… during the summer.

During describes the period in which something happens. We can also say:

in the summer / autumn / winter / spring.

See Reference Section 19.1 for more on time prepositions.

… in the first quarter of the year.
… in the second quarter.

Note also:

in the first / second half of the year.

… to remain stable.
… to pick up.

Note this language:

We expect / don't expect sales to …

… rise.	*… fall.*	*… go up.*	*… go down.*
… increase.	*… decrease.*	*… peak.*	*… reach a low point.*

If the dollar falls in value, we will sell more abroad.
We'll be able to export more if the dollar falls.

Note these examples of the First Conditional.

Notice that we do not say: *If the Government will fall …* **or** *if there will be a fall.*

See Reference Section 4.3.

Practice

Forecasts

1 Match the speaker with the graph described. Then make similar forecasts about your own company.

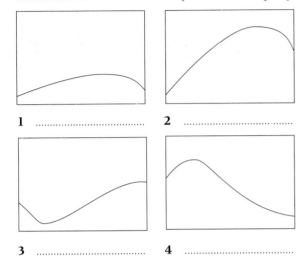

1 ....

2 ....

3 ....

4 ....

The First Conditional

2 Put the verbs in brackets in the correct tense.

A: There are two possible candidates for the sales manager's job in Brazil. Dacia Frio and Derek Hayward. If we **a** ......*choose*...... (choose) Dacia Frio, we **b** .... (have) someone who is young and inexperienced, but full of ideas. On the other hand, if we **c** .... (decide) to appoint Derek Hayward, we **d** .... (have) a person who knows South America better than anyone.

B: What do you think Dacia **e** .... (do) if we **f** .... (not offer) her the job?

A: I think that we **g** .... (may lose) her if she **h** .... (not offer) it. She is very ambitious. Another company **i** .... (offer) her something interesting.

B: And what about Derek?

A: I know he wants the job, but I'm not sure that he **j** .... (stay) with the company even if he **k** .... (not get) it.

Phrases for forecasting

3 Tick the phrase in column B which is nearest in meaning to the phrase in column A.

A	**B**
a Sales fell.	Sales decreased. ✔ Sales remained stable.
b Prices are likely to go up.	Prices will probably go up. Prices might go up.
c We forecast a 10% increase.	We predict a 10% increase. We hope there will be a 10% increase.
d We expect sales to increase considerably.	We expect sales to increase slightly. We expect sales to increase substantially.

Periods of time

4 Complete the sentences with a suitable word or phrase.

e.g. We will continue to expand in the short .*term*..

a Sales will fall back in the third ....

b We plan to close our factory in Scotland in the second .... of the year.

c We will continue to expand .... the medium term.

d We are expecting things to remain stable during the ....

e We believe .... will pick up in the spring.

f We plan to open three new stores during the coming ....

UNIT 32

Trade enquiries

Some useful phrases

Listen to the recording and repeat

Can I speak to the person who deals with trade enquiries?

Can you put me through to the department which handles telephone sales?

Can I speak to the person I spoke to earlier?

I am (I'm) enquiring about videophones.

I would (I'd) like some information on your new range.

We are (We're) looking for something which is economic to run.

We need something that is easy to install.

You probably need an XL 70.

The XL 70 should suit you.

You may need a more reliable product.

It might not be competitive enough for our market.

Can you send me your specifications?

Could I have a price list?

I will (I'll) send you the details.

You can download a brochure from our website.

What sort of price do you sell it for?

How much would you sell it to us for?

Is there a volume discount?

Where shall I send the information?

Could you fax it to me?

Mark it for my attention.

Study notes

... the person who deals with trade enquiries.
... the department which handles telephone sales.
See Reference Section 13.4.

... easy to install.
Notice also these examples:
It is difficult to understand.   *It is expensive to maintain.*
It is economic to run.

You may need a more reliable product.
It might not be competitive enough for our market.
May and *might* both express possibility:
We may/might (not) get the contract.
She may/might (not) be able to help.
Note that *may* is also used in asking for and giving permission:
– May I use your phone?   *– Of course you may.*
See also Reference Section 9.2.

... competitive enough for our market.
Enough stands after adjectives and adverbs:
competitive enough, well enough.
It stands before nouns:
enough information, enough money.
See also Reference Section 15.4.

Can you send me your specifications?
Notice that you can also say:
Can you send them to me?
Note also:
Fax me the details.   *Send it as an attachment.*
Email it to me.   *Send me the web page.*

Practice

Telephone enquiries

1 Listen to the recording and match the questions/prompts with the responses. Then write down what you hear and check the audioscript.

   a Can I speak to the person who deals with trade enquiries? ☐

   b Can you put me through to the department that handles telephone sales? ☐

   c Can you send me the specifications? ☐

   i I'll send you the details.

   ii I'm putting you through.

   iii Hold on, I'll try to connect you.

enough

2 Add *enough* to these sentences.

   e.g. It isn't light to carry.

      It isn't light enough to carry.

   a Have you got time?

   b I see I didn't order headed notepaper.

   c I don't think we have space to store it.

   d Your prices aren't competitive.

   e The other model doesn't sell well.

   f Our customers don't have money to buy products like these.

   g Have you got publicity material?

who, which, what

3 i Delete the relative pronouns (*who, which, that*) where possible.

   e.g. The person ~~that~~ I spoke to said it would be OK.

   a The person who deals with this is out.
   b The person that you spoke to is not at his desk.
   c The line which you want is engaged.
   d Do you have one that is cheaper?
   e The item which you ordered is ready for collection.
   f We are looking for a product that is versatile and easy to use.
   g I work for a company which has strong links with the local community.
   h I do a job that is demanding, but highly paid.

   ii Complete the sentences below, using information from the box.

> it is economical to run   you want
> he/she handles telephone sales   it deals with new enquiries
> it manufactures computer screens ✓   he knows about this
> you need him/her ✓   you sent them to me

   e.g. (She works for a company.)
     She works for a company which/that manufactures computer screens.

     (The person is out of the office at the moment.)
     The person (who/that) you need is out of the office at the moment.

   a (We are looking for something.)

   b (I'm afraid I can't find the man.)

   c (Can you put me through to the department?)

   d (Can I check the details?)

   e (Can I speak to the person?)

   f (The extension is engaged.)

A trade enquiry

4 Read the dialogue and fill in the gaps, using phrases from the box.

a brochure	a price list	good value
enquiring about	on your new range	that is both
who deals with ✓	too expensive	

A: Can I speak to the person **a** *who deals with* trade enquiries?

B: I'm putting you through.

C: Trade Enquiries.

A: I'm **b** .... videophones. I'd like some information **c** ....

C: Certainly. What exactly are you looking for?

A: Well, we're looking for something **d** .... user-friendly and **e** .... for money.

C: The new range should suit you. Have you got **f** .... ?

A: Yes, they look very good. But I'm concerned about the pricing. They may be **g** .... for our market. I need the specifications and **h** ....

C: Give me your email address and I'll send you the details.

A: Thanks.

may, might, will, etc.

5 Write examples of the following, using a dictionary if necessary.

Use words such as *might, may, will, won't, certain to,* etc.

e.g. … something that you think will definitely happen.

I think we'll (definitely) get the Millfield contract.

a … something that everyone thinks is unlikely that you believe may happen.

....

b … something that is generally expected that you think might not happen.

....

c … something that will certainly not happen.

....

d … something that you believe is sure to happen.

....

e … something that you are hoping for that may not happen.

....

f … something that certainly will not happen.

....

UNIT 33

Clarification and adjustment

Some useful phrases

Listen to the recording and repeat

I think there is (there's) a mistake in your invoice.
I think the total is wrong.
I think you have (you've) overcharged us.
I think the total should be $700.

Did not (Didn't) we order five, not ten?
Is not (Isn't) the unit price 3 euros?
We ordered ten – you sent five.
Are they out of stock?

Could you check your records?
Just a moment, I will (I'll) get the details.
I have your order in front of me.
According to this, you ordered five.

I am (I'm) afraid we made a mistake.
You've got an out-of-date price list.
I'll send you an up-to-date catalogue.

Will you send us a credit note?
When can you collect the goods?
How soon can you deliver the replacements?

Shall I send you the new model instead?
Shall I send you the new model …
… instead of the LS 24?
… in place of the other one?

Please accept our apologies.
It was our mistake.
It is (It's) OK. It does not (doesn't) matter.
I'm very sorry about this.

Study notes

Notice the pronunciation of *ea* in *instead*. Compare this with the pronunciation of *ea* in *please*.

Didn't we order five, not ten?
We use negative questions when we believe that what we are saying is true.
Isn't the unit price £3?
Aren't you John Smith?
See also Reference Section 16.3.

I'm afraid we made a mistake.
Note these other common expressions using *make*:
make money, make a profit, make a loss, make a suggestion, make a decision, make arrangements, make a phone call, make coffee.
Compare these with some common expressions using *do*:
do some work, do some typing, do the cooking, do the accounts, do business, do something, do someone a favour, do better.
See also Reference Section 20.2.

… instead of the LS 24?
… in place of the other one?
Note the use of *instead of* and *in place of*. They have a similar meaning. *Instead* can also be used as an adverb:
Shall I send you the new model instead?
(not *Shall I send you the new model in place?*)
See Reference Section 20.18.

I'm very sorry about this.
Note how the use of *very* and *indeed* in some of these apologies makes them stronger:
– *I'm sorry. It's our mistake.*
– *That's/It's OK.*
– *We are very sorry.*
– *It doesn't matter.*
– *We are very sorry indeed.*
– *Really, it's OK – don't worry!*

Negative questions

1 Make negative questions, then listen to the recording and tick ☑ the response.

e.g. I thought you stocked the blue ones.   Yes   No
..... *Don't you stock blue ones?* .....   ☐   ☑

a I think you ordered eight.
....   ☐   ☐

b I understand the price is $8.
....   ☐   ☐

c Am I right in thinking you're John Kaye?
....   ☐   ☐

d I thought you ordered CFL 18s.
....   ☐   ☐

e I think you said Tuesday.
....   ☐   ☐

do, make

2 Write sentences using *do* or *make*.

e.g. (money) ..... *How much money did you make on that deal?* .....

a (arrangements)
....

b (a deal)
....

c (a reservation)
....

d (a suggestion)
....

e (a phone call)
....

f (a loss)
....

g (some good contracts)
....

h (more business)
....

instead of, in place of

3 Replace *instead of* with *in place of* where possible.

e.g. We bought a second-hand machine ~~instead of~~ *in place of* a new one.

no change
Instead of buying a new machine, we bought a second-hand one.

The prices were too high so we bought a second-hand one instead.
no change

a Shall I send you the new model instead of the LS 24?
....

b Instead of buying a warehouse, we are renting one.
....

c There were no Toyotas available, so I hired a Honda instead.
....

d We ordered the green model instead of the blue one.
....

e Instead of sending a replacement, could you send us a credit note?
....

f Could you send us three boxes of PL 40s instead of the PL 50s that were delivered by mistake?
....

Checking details

4 Fill in the gaps in the dialogue, using words and phrases from the box.

according to	in connection with ✓	the details
overcharged	out-of-date	your records
the unit price		

A: I'm calling **a** *in connection with* your invoice number ZL701.

B: How can I help?

A: I think you've made a mistake. I think you have **b** .... us. The total should be €249, not €291. Could you check **c** .... ?

B: Just a moment, I'll get **d** .... Right, I have the invoice in front of me. **e** .... this, you ordered 300 units.

A: That's right, but isn't **f** .... 83 cents?

B: No, it's 97 cents. I'm afraid you have an **g** .... price list. Our prices went up in November.

A: I'm sorry. It's our mistake.

Apologies

5 i How many apologies can you write using the words in the box in different combinations?

am	apologise	do	I	indeed
really	so	sorry	very	

e.g. *I am sorry.*

ii How many responses to apologies can you write using the words in the box in different combinations?

doesn't	don't	is	it
matter	mention	OK	please
really	that	worry	

e.g. *That's OK.*

Sorting out problems

6 Identify the three problems discussed in the dialogues from the list of five problems.

Problem	Dialogue
a overcharged	....
b short order	....
c out of stock	....
d out-of-date price list	....
e late delivery	....

Dialogue 1

– Didn't we order 24 TX 400s?
– Yes, you did, but I'm afraid we've run out.
– And when will you have them?
– Not till next week. I could send you TX 300s instead.
– Are they the same price?
– They're a little cheaper.
– OK, when can you deliver the replacements?
– Tomorrow.

Dialogue 2

– Have you got our order number AB317 there?
– Yes, I have it in front of me. According to this, you ordered 200 units.
– That's right, but you only delivered 100.
– Oh. Are you sure?
– Yes I am. Please check the dispatch note.
– Oh yes, I'm sorry about that.
– That's OK.
– How soon can you send the missing goods?
– This afternoon, if you like.
– That's fine.

Dialogue 3

– I'm calling about your invoice ZX017.
– What's the problem?
– I think you charged us to much. Didn't we order ten boxes?
– Let me check my records. Yes, you did.
– And that's what you delivered. But you charged us for twenty.

UNIT 34

Making bookings

Some useful phrases

Listen to the recording and repeat

I have four clients to entertain on the 27th.
We can offer you tickets for all the main events.
Do you have any tickets for the opera?
We have some available in the stalls.
I would (I'd) rather have a box.
We would (We'd) prefer to go on the Wednesday.

I'd like to book two tickets …
… for the game on the 26th.
Do you have two tickets …
… for tonight's performance?

    game   match   performance   show

We have two seats in row G – seats 45 and 46.
They are (They're) in the middle.

    in the middle   at the front   at the back

They are €50 each.
Box A is available.
That is (That's) €600 for the night.
It does not (doesn't) include food or drinks.
Refreshments are extra.

The show starts at 7.30pm.
It finishes at 10.30.

I will (I'll) contact you as soon as I know the details.
I'll let you know when I have the tickets.
Please let me know if there are any problems.

Study notes

Note the common contraction of *would* to *'d*.
Listen again and practise:
I'd rather have a box.   *I'd like to book two tickets.*

I have four clients to entertain …
Notice these examples:
I have some work to do.   *I have a lot to do.*
We have some clients to visit.

I'd rather have a box.
We'd prefer to go on the Wednesday.
Compare *would prefer* and *would rather*.
We'd rather go on Thursday.   *I'd prefer to go on Saturday.*
She may prefer to go to the opera.   *Would you rather have a cup of coffee?*

tonight's performance
Notice how the possessive *'s* is used in these examples:
Tuesday's show   next week's game   last Monday's meeting
See also Reference Section 12.4.

The show starts at 7.30pm.
Note these examples of the Simple Present tense:
The play begins at 7.30 and finishes at 10.15.
What time does the bank close this afternoon?
The next train arrives at ten o'clock.
See Reference Section 2.3.

I'll contact you as soon as I know the details.
Notice that we say *as soon as I know* (not *as soon as I will know*).
Note these other examples:
I'll call you when he arrives.
(not … *when he will arrive*)
I'll let you know if there are any problems.
(not *if there will be any problems*)
See Reference Section 3.5.

Practice

The Simple Present tense for timetables

1 Listen and match the details.

a	A play	**i**	8pm – 10.15pm
b	A film	**ii**	14.00 – 16.20
c	A match	**iii**	7.30pm – 10pm
d	A train	**iv**	2.30pm – 4.15pm

Vocabulary extension

2 Complete the sets with words from the box. Use a dictionary if you need to.

musical ✓	box	crowd	player
pitch	rugby	show	wrestling

a	concert	opera	*musical*
b	circle	stalls	....
c	match	performance	....
d	football	baseball	....
e	racing	boxing	....
f	course	court	....
g	actor	performance	....
h	spectator	audience	....

when, as soon as + will

3 Put the verbs in brackets in the right form.

e.g. When the tickets ..... *arrive* ...... (arrive), ... *I will let* .... (let) you know.

a I .... (contact) you when I .... (have) the information.

b If there .... (be) no tickets, I .... (call) you.

c I .... (confirm) the booking as soon as I .... (get) your quote.

d When the contract .... (be) signed, we .... (pay) the deposit.

e I .... (get) back to you if there .... (be) any problems.

A call to a hospitality company

4 Fill in the gaps in the dialogue using the words and phrases from the box.

confirm	for the 27th	include	in the middle
receive	row	the main events	to entertain ✓

A: I have some clients **a** *to entertain* on the 27th.

B: We have tickets for all **b** ....

A: Do you have tickets for Wimbledon?

B: Yes, we have seats for Centre Court on most days.

A: OK. I'd like four tickets **c** ....

B: We have seats in **d** .... G, seats 25 to 28. They're **e** ....

A: How much are they?

B: £80 each.

A: What does that **f** .... ?

B: It includes the seat price and parking.

A: That's fine. I'll **g** .... the booking as soon as I **h** .... the details in writing.

would prefer (to), would rather

5 Write true sentences about yourself, using the prompts and *would prefer (to)/would rather*.

e.g. go to a football match / watch hockey

..... *I'd prefer to go to a football match than watch hockey.* .....

drive/go by train

..... *I'd rather drive than go by train.* .....

a go to the theatre / watch a video (prefer) ....

b read a book / listen to the radio (rather) ....

c live in the country / in the city (prefer) ....

d play tennis / watch tennis (rather) ....

UNIT 35

When things go wrong

Some useful phrases

Listen to the recording and repeat

I am (I'm) afraid there is a problem with your booking.

The flight is overbooked.

The restaurant is fully booked.

The hotel has no vacancies.

The airline called. They said that the flight was cancelled.

The hotel called. They said they had no double rooms left.

They said that they could only offer two singles.

They said that they could not (couldn't) offer you a double till the 21st.

They said they were very sorry.

But we booked.

We confirmed it in writing.

They say they have no record of our booking.

They say they did not (didn't) receive our confirmation.

Is there another flight?

Are there any seats left on a later flight?

What about the following day?

What are the alternatives?

We had (We'd) better try another hotel.

You had (You'd) better book somewhere else.

I had (I'd) better call them and sort it out.

Study notes

The flight is overbooked.

Notice how *over* can be added to certain verbs:

to overwork   e.g. *I am overworked.*

to overprice   e.g. *These goods are overpriced.*

to overpay   e.g. *They overpay their staff.*

They said that the flight was cancelled.
They said they had no double rooms left.

Note also these examples of reported speech:

They said that the flight is cancelled.

They said they have no double rooms left.

Note that *that* is optional:

He said that they would have a table at eight.

He said they would have a table at eight.

See Reference Section 6 for further details of reported speech.

... they could only offer two singles.

Note the uses of *only* in these examples:

The restaurant only opens in the evening.

The plane is only half-full.

See Reference Section 20.19.

a double (room)

Note also:

a twin room/twin rooms (two beds)

a single room   a single bed   a double bed

We'd better try another hotel.

Note that the meaning of *had better* is similar to *should*. The same form is used to talk about the present and future:

We'd better do it now.

I'd better do it next week.

See also Reference Section 20.8.

Reported speech

1 Listen to the information and write it as reported speech.

e.g. *He said there were no vacancies in first class on Friday's flight.*

a ....

b ....

c ....

d ....

e ....

f ....

only, probably, also

2 Add *only, also* or *probably* to the sentences.

e.g. (only) The restaurant opens in the evening.

The restaurant only opens in the evening.

a (only) The plane is half full.

....

b (probably) They will change the booking if you go to the office.

....

c (probably) The sales conference will be in May.

....

d (also) The promotions manager has the number.

....

e (only) We have two days left.

....

had better

3 Match the problem with the advice or action required.

a The hotel has no record of your booking. ☐ iii

b There are no seats on the flight. ☐

c It's raining. ☐

d The restaurant is fully booked. ☐

e I've got a pain in my back. ☐

f The restaurant is on the outskirts of town. ☐

i You'd better take an umbrella.

ii We'd better go by taxi.

iii I'd better call them and sort it out.

iv You'd better go and see the nurse.

v We'd better try another airline.

vi We'd better book somewhere else.

Passing on information

4 Fill in the gaps in the dialogue, using words from the box.

of	made	to ✓	with
told	by	received	

A: Did you call the restaurant a ....to.... say we'd be a bit late?

B: I did, and I'm afraid there's a problem b .... our booking.

A: What's that?

B: They c .... me that they can't find any record d .... it.

A: But we e .... the reservation on their website last week.

B: Yes, we did, and we f .... confirmation g .... email. But I didn't keep a copy of the email!

UNIT 36

Sorting things out

Listen to the recording and repeat

Where can I get my suit cleaned?

Where can I get this document typed?

There is (There's) a secretarial bureau on the third floor.

Why isn't the lift working?

What is (What's) wrong with the air conditioning?

It is (It's) out of order.

An engineer is working on it.

I am (I'm) calling from Room 204.

There's no hot water.

The room needs cleaning.

There's something wrong with the shower.

I had to make the bed myself.

We had to clean the bath ourselves.

Our toilet isn't working.

Our toilet still isn't working.

Have you contacted the maintenance engineer yet?

I was having a shower when the water went off.

I was calling my office when I was cut off.

Were you watching TV when he called?

Yes, we were.   No, we were not (weren't).

What is (What's) going on?

I will (I'll) send someone to your room.

I'll contact the manager immediately.

We'll sort it out for you.

Study notes

Where can I get my suit cleaned?
Note the construction *get* + noun + past participle.
Note that we can also use *have* instead of *get*:
Where can I get this letter typed?   Where can I have my car repaired?
See Reference Section 20.7.

The room needs cleaning.
Note the negative and interrogative forms:
Does it need cleaning?   It doesn't need cleaning.
See Reference Section 8.

I had to make the bed myself.
We had to clean the bath ourselves.
Note this use of the reflexive pronoun (*myself, ourselves*) for emphasis.
See Reference Section 13.3.

… still isn't working.
Have you contacted the maintenance engineer yet?
Note the use of *still* and *yet* in these examples:
The TV is still out of order.   The room still needs cleaning.
It still isn't working.   Is it ready yet?
We haven't finished yet.
See Reference Section 20.10.

I was having a shower when …
I was calling my office when …
Note these examples of the Past Continuous tense.
Note the difference in meaning between:
When the doorbell rang, I was sitting down.
When the doorbell rang, I stood up.
See Reference Section 2.6.

Reflexive pronouns

1 Listen and write the sentences a–e, then match them with i–v.

a (bath) _The bath needed cleaning._ ☑

b (the document) .... ☐

c (the cases) .... ☐

d (my suit) .... ☐

e (the bed) .... ☐

i .... (myself)

ii .... (herself)

iii .... (himself)

iv .... (themselves)

v _We cleaned it ourselves._ (ourselves)

The Past Continuous tense

2 Answer the questions using the information in the table.

	Tom	Mary
8.30 – 9.00	Wrote report.	Drove to work.
10.30 – 10.45	Had coffee.	Read mail.
11.00 – 12.00	Talked to MD.	Visited clients.
12.30 – 1.15	Made phone calls.	Had lunch.

e.g. What was Tom doing at half past eleven?
He was talking to the MD.

a Was Mary visiting clients at 10.30?

....

b What was she doing at one o'clock?

....

c Was Tom having coffee at 10.35?

....

d Was Tom driving to work at 8.40?

....

e What was he doing just before lunch?

....

To get something done

3 Put the words in the correct order. Then match the sentences a–e with sentences i–v.

a cleaned/where/a/suit/get/can/I?
Where can I get a suit cleaned? i

b get/washed/can/I/my/shirts/where?

.... ☐

c of/report/some/get/where/made/can/I/ copies/this?

.... ☐

d I/film/get/can/where/a/developed?

.... ☐

e a/translated/get/can/where/I/letter?

.... ☐

i looking/dry cleaner's/still/for/I'm/a
I'm still looking for a dry cleaner's.

ii can't/camera shop/find/I/a/still

....

iii open/isn't/laundry/yet/the

....

iv the/have/business/service/centre/do/address/ of/the/still/you?

....

v that/yet/found/I/photocopier/a/haven't/ works

....

A complaint

4 Read this complaint. What four promises did Mr Agit make and then not keep?

The four promises:

1 ....
2 ....
3 ....
4 ....

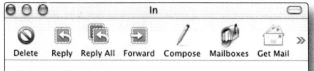

Subject: Conference facilities

Dear Mr Agit

I am writing to complain about the conference facilities we hired from you on the 14th of this month.

In your letter of 21st February, you assured me the room would be large enough for our needs, and that it would be ready for use at 10am.

The room you provided was much too small for us to use and the alternative we moved to had to be cleaned before we could occupy it. The start of our conference was delayed for fifty minutes. In addition, the second room was not air-conditioned, as agreed.

Finally, the refreshments you supplied did not arrive at the agreed times, and they were of very poor quality.

I hope the invoice you send us will reflect these circumstances. Please contact me if you wish to discuss any of the above points.

Yours sincerely

C L Walsh

Reference section: index

1 SPECIAL VERBS

1.1 be

Present tense

I am (I'm)	I am not	(I'm not)	am I?
you are (you're)	you are not	(you're not/ you aren't)	are you?
he is (he's)	he is not	(he's not/ he isn't)	is he?
she is (she's)	she is not	(she's not/ she isn't)	is she?
it is (it's)	it is not	(it's not/ it isn't)	is it?
we are (we're)	we are not	(we're not/ we aren't)	are we?
you are (you're)	you are not	(you're not/ you aren't)	are you?
they are (they're)	they are not	(they're not/ they aren't)	are they?

e.g. I**'m** from France.

I**'m** thirty-seven. (not *I have thirty-seven.*)

She **isn't** in the sales department.

They **aren't** in the office.

Are you an engineer?   Yes, I **am**.

Is he a sales rep?   No, he **isn't**.

Past tense

I was	I was not	(I wasn't)	was I?
you were	you were not	(you weren't)	were you?
he, etc. was	she, etc. was not	(she wasn't)	was it, etc.?
we were	we were not	(we weren't)	were we?
you were	you were not	(you weren't)	were you?
they were	they were not	(they weren't)	were they?

e.g. The weather **was** very nice.

The people **were** very friendly.

The journey **wasn't** very long.

The hotels **weren't** very good.

Were you at the conference?   No, I **wasn't**.

Were they in the office?   Yes, they **were**.

1.2 there is

Present tense

there is	there is not	(there isn't)	is there?
there are	there are not	(there aren't)	are there?

There is and *there are* are used to talk about people, things and situations that exist now.

e.g. **There's** a car park in the basement.

There aren't any shops near here.

Is there a bank near here?   Yes, **there is**.

Past tense

there was	there was not	(there wasn't)	was there?
there were	there were not	(there weren't)	were there?

There was and *there were* are used to talk about people, things and situations that existed in the past.

e.g. **There were** some warehouses along the river.

There weren't any banks near the hotel.

Were there any problems?   No, **there weren't**.

Note that *there used to be* can also be used to describe past situations (see section 20.9).

1.3 have

Present tense

I have	I do not (don't) have	do I have?
you have	you do not (don't) have	do you have?
he, etc. has	she, etc. does not (doesn't) have	does it, etc. have?
we have	we do not (don't) have	do we have?
you have	you do not (don't) have	do you have?
they have	they do not (don't) have	do they have?

e.g. It **has** ten floors.

We **have** a canteen.

He **doesn't have** a secretary.

They **don't have** a car park.

Do you **have** a translation unit?   Yes, we **do**.

Does your company **have** a canteen?   No, it **doesn't**.

1.4 have got

Have got means the same as *have*. *Have got* in the Present tense is very common in spoken British English. *Have* is more common in American English.

Present tense

I have (I've) got	I have not (haven't) got	have I got?
you have (you've) got	you have not (haven't) got	have you got?
he, etc. has (he's) got	she, etc. has not (hasn't) got	has it, etc. got?
we have (we've) got	we have not (haven't) got	have we got?
you have (you've) got	you have not (haven't) got	have you got?
they have (they've) got	they have not (haven't) got	have they got?

e.g. I've **got** a new computer.

They **haven't got** many orders.

Have you **got** a fax?   Yes, we **have**.

Past tense

I had	I did not (didn't) have	did I have?
you had	you did not (didn't) have	did you have?
he, etc. had	she, etc. did not (didn't) have	did it, etc. have?
we had	we did not (didn't) have	did we have?
you had	you did not (didn't) have	did you have?
they had	they did not (didn't) have	did they have?

e.g. We **had** a lot of problems last year.
They **had** a working breakfast.
I **didn't have** all the information.
Did you **have** a good trip?   No, I **didn't**.
Did they **have** lunch with you?   Yes, they **did**.

2 ORDINARY VERBS

2.1 *Simple Present*

I work	I do not (don't) work	do I work?
you work	you do not (don't) work	do you work?
he, etc. works	she, etc. does not (doesn't) work	does it, etc. work?
we work	we do not (don't) work	do we work?
you work	you do not (don't) work	do you work?
they work	they do not (don't) work	do they work?

e.g. He **works** for a bank.
I **live** in York.
She **doesn't like** her new job.
We **don't work** on the manufacturing side.
Does he often go abroad?   Yes, he **does**.

Spelling of *he/she/it* forms

most verbs:	get	→	gets
	want	→	wants
	live	→	lives
verbs ending in consonant + *-y*:	try	→	tries
	worry	→	worries
verbs ending in *-ch*, *-sh* or *-s*:	watch	→	watches
	wish	→	wishes
	miss	→	misses
irregular:	have	→	has
	do	→	does
	go	→	goes

2.2 *Present Continuous*

I am (I'm) staying	I am not (I'm not) staying
you are (you're) staying	you are not (you're not/you aren't) staying
he, etc. is (he's) staying	she, etc. is not (we're not/you aren't) staying
we are (we're) staying	we are not (we're not/we aren't) staying
you are (you're) staying	you are not (you're not/you aren't) staying
they are (they're) staying	they are not (they're not/they aren't) staying

am I staying?
are you staying?
is it, etc. staying?
are we staying?
are they staying?

e.g. Bill'**s working** in the Middle East.
We'**re developing** a new model.
It **isn't photocopying** very well.
They **aren't having** lunch.
Are you **waiting** for a taxi?   No, I'**m not**.
Is business **going** well?   Yes, it **is**.

Spelling of infinitive + *-ing* forms

most verbs:	work	→	working
	eat	→	eating
verbs ending in *-e*:	write	→	writing
	make	→	making
short verbs ending in one vowel + one consonant:	stop	→	stopping
	plan	→	planning
	fit	→	fitting
verbs ending in *-e*:	lie	'	lying
	die	→	dying

2.3 *Simple Present vs. Present Continuous*

We use the Simple Present to talk about:

– things that are true all the time

e.g. What **does** your company **do**?
The company **makes** computers.

– things that happen often, usually, sometimes, etc.

e.g. I usually **arrive** at the office at 9am.
I often **work** on Saturday.

We use the Present Continuous to talk about:

– things that are happening at the moment of speaking

   e.g. I'**m talking** to John.
       It's **raining**.

– things that are happening or changing these days

   e.g. What **are** you **working** on?
       They'**re installing** a new security system.

– situations that are temporary

Compare: **I am staying** at the Grand Hotel.   (temporary)
with: He lives in Monaco.   (all the time)

– plans for the future (see also section 3)

   e.g. We'**re going** to Geneva next month.
       What **are** you **doing** on Friday morning?

We use the Simple Present or the Present Continuous for some verbs with no change in meaning (e.g. *feel, look, hurt, hope*):

You **look** well.   **or**   You **are looking** well.
I **feel** tired.   **or**   I **am feeling** tired.
My head **hurts**.   **or**   My head **is hurting**.

2.4 Non-Continuous verbs

With some verbs, we usually use simple tense, not Continuous tenses:

– verbs of thinking (e.g. *believe, think* (= *believe*), *agree, understand, know, remember, forget*)

   e.g. I **believe** they're in Rome.   (not *I am believing* …)
       I **think** he's at home.   (not *I am thinking* …)
       I **understand** you're leaving tomorrow afternoon.
                                       (not *I am understanding* …)

– verbs of feeling (e.g. *want, wish, like, love, hate*)

   e.g. I **want** to do a course in marketing.
       (not *I am wanting* …)
       I **don't like** espresso coffee. (not *I am not liking* …)

– verbs of possession (e.g. *have, have got, own, belong*)

   e.g. He **has** a new computer. (not *He is having* …)
       They **don't own** the fleet of lorries. (not *They are not owning* …)
       It **belongs** to me. (not *It is belonging to me* …)

2.5 Simple Past

I started you started he, etc. started we started you started they started	I did not (didn't) start you did not (didn't) start she, etc. did not (didn't) start we did not (didn't) start you did not (didn't) start they did not (didn't) start	did I start? did you start? did it, etc. start? did we start? did you start? did they start?

e.g. Jane **went** to Paris by plane.
   John **didn't call** me. (not *didn't called* …)
   Did you **like** living in London? Yes, I **did**.
   (not *Yes, I liked* …)

Spelling of regular past tense

most regular verbs:	work → worked develop → developed
verbs ending in -*e*:	like → liked phone → phoned
verbs ending in consonant + -*y*:	try → tried marry → married
short verbs ending in one vowel + one consonant	stop → stopped plan → planned fit → fitted

2.6 Past Continuous

I was writing	I was not (wasn't) writing	was I writing?
you were writing	you were not (weren't) writing	were you writing?
he, etc. was writing	she, etc. was not (weren't) writing	was it, etc. writing?
we were writing	we were not (weren't) writing	were we writing?
you were writing	you were not (weren't) writing	were you writing?
they were writing	they were not (weren't) writing	were they writing?

We use the Past Continuous to talk about:

– the background situation at the moment something happened

   e.g. I **was having** lunch when you called yesterday.
       It **was snowing** when I left.

– what was happening at a particular time

   e.g. What **were** you **doing** at 16.30 yesterday?
       This time last year, I **was working** in Osaka.

2.7 Simple Past vs. Past Continuous

Notice the difference between:

   When the doorbell **rang**, I **was sitting** down.
   When the doorbell **rang**, I **got up**.

In the first sentence, *sitting down* tells us about the background situation when something happened (*the doorbell rang*). In the second sentence, one action (*the doorbell rang*) is followed by another (*I got up*).

2.8 Simple Present Perfect

I have (I've) visited	I have not (haven't) visited	have I visited?
you have (you've) visited	you have not (haven't) visited	have you visited?
he, etc. has (he's) visited	she, etc. has not (hasn't) visited	has it, etc. visited?
we have (we've) visited	we have not (haven't) visited	have we visited?
you have (you've) visited	you have not (haven't) visited	have you visited?
they have (they've) visited	they have not (haven't) visited	have they visited?

We use the Simple Perfect to talk about:

– experiences

e.g. **Have** you ever **visited** New York?
Yes, I **have**. / No, I **haven't**.

– unfinished past

e.g. I**'ve worked** for Datalab for/since …
They **haven't finished** yet.

– developments

e.g. Prices **have risen** since last year.
The number of complaints **has fallen**.

– news

e.g. They **have closed** the design department.
The President **has** just **died**.

– current information

e.g. I **have** just **seen** Tony Kwon.
I haven't finished work yet.

In US English, the Simple Past is often used for news and current information.

e.g. They **closed** the design department.
I just **saw** Tony Kwon.
The President just **died**.
I **didn't finish** the work yet.

We do not use the Present Perfect to talk about:

– a finished time

e.g. **I changed** my job **last month**.
(not *I have changed my job last month*.)
I saw Tosca **four years ago**.
(not *I have seen Tosca four years ago*.)
I visited Mr Schmidt **when** I was in Frankfurt.
(not *I've visited Mr Schmidt when I was in Frankfurt*.)

2.9 Present Perfect Continuous

I have (I've) been waiting	I have not (haven't) been waiting
you have (you've) been waiting	you have not (haven't) been waiting
he, etc. has (he's) been waiting	she, etc. has not (hasn't) been waiting
we have (we've) been waiting	we have not (haven't) been waiting
you have (you've) been waiting	you have not (haven't) been waiting
they have (they've) been waiting	they have not (haven't) been waiting

have I been waiting?
have you been waiting?
has it, etc. been waiting?
have we been waiting?
have you been waiting?
have they been waiting?

We use the Present Perfect Continuous to talk about:

– things which started in the past and are still happening or have only just finished

e.g. I**'ve been trying** to contact you all morning.
She **hasn't been answering** the phone.
Have you been receiving our messages?

– how long something has gone on

e.g. **How long have** you **been working** here?
He's **been working** on the project **since** January.
I**'ve been waiting** for an hour.

2.10 Simple Present Perfect vs. Present Perfect Continuous

Sometimes the difference between the two tenses is clear.

e.g. I**'ve written** the report you wanted.
I**'ve been writing** reports all morning.

In the first sentence, we use the Simple Present Perfect because we are giving news of a completed action. In the second sentence, we use the Present Perfect Continuous to show that an action has continued over a period of time. We are not talking about a completed action, but about the process.

Sometimes the difference is small and is only a matter of emphasis.

e.g. I **have lived** in Budapest for three years.
I **have been living** in Budapest for three years.

The first sentence gives the facts. The second sentence gives more emphasis to the extended period of time.

Some verbs are normally only used in the Simple Present Perfect:

– verbs of thinking, e.g. *believe*, *think* (= believe), *understand*, *know*

   e.g. I've known about the problem for a month.
   (not *I've been knowing about the problem for a month*.)

– verbs of possession, e.g. *have*, *have got*, *own*, *belong*

   e.g. I've had this car for years.
   (not *I've been having this car for years*.)

3 TALKING ABOUT THE FUTURE

We use several different tenses to talk about the future.

3.1 *Simple Present (programme, timetable)*

e.g. What time **does** your plane leave?
    We **leave** Paris at 10.30 on Saturday.

3.2 *Present Continuous (plans, arrangements)*

e.g. **Are** you **doing** anything this evening?
    I'**m leaving** on Tuesday.
    I'**m staying** in Madrid for three days.

3.3 going to + *infinitive (intentions, plans)*

e.g. What **are** you **going to do** in Madrid?
    I **am going to meet** some important clients.
    I'**m not going to visit** Moscow this year.

3.4 will *(sudden decisions, promises, predictions, offers)*

e.g. I'**ll call** the bank. (a sudden decision made at the moment of speaking)
    You **will have** the money tomorrow.   (a promise)
    I expect the money **will turn up** tomorrow. (a prediction)
    I'**ll carry** the heavy box.   (an offer)

Notice that both *will* and the Present tense can be used for timetable business events (visits, conferences, etc.):

    How long **will** you be here for?
    I'**ll** be here until Friday.
or How long **are** you here for?
    I **am** here until Friday.

3.5 when, as soon as *and* while

We use a Simple Present Tense form after *when, as soon as* and *while* when they refer to the future.

e.g. **When I have** details, I'll phone you.
    (not *When I will have the details …*)

They'll let us know **as soon as** the tickets are ready.
(Not … *as soon as the tickets will be ready*.)
Will you have any free time **while** you **are** here?
(Not … *while you will be here*.)

4 CONDITIONALS (*IF*)

4.1 *Position of* if

It is usually possible for the *if* part of the sentence to go either first or second.

e.g. **If** you switch on the engine, the green lamp goes on.
    The green lamp goes on **if** you switch on the engine.
    If there's a cut in rates we'll be able to invest more.
    We'll be able to invest more **if** there is a cut in rates.

4.2 *The Zero Conditional*

We can use *if* to talk about the general conditions. We use the Simple Present tense for both verbs.

e.g. **If** you **switch** on the engine, the green lamp **goes on**.
    If something **goes wrong**, the red lamp **goes on**.

4.3 *The First Conditional*

We can use *if* to talk about situations we think may happen in the future. We use a Simple Present tense for the verb with *if*, and *will* for the other verb.

e.g. **If** the rupee **is devalued**, we **will be** more competitive.
    (not *If the rupee will be devalued …*)
    If there's a cut in rates, we **will be** able to invest more.
    (not *If there will be …*)

5 THE PASSIVE

Simple Present Passive

subject	*am/is/are*	past participle
The customer	is	contacted
The customer	isn't	contacted
The forms	are	signed
The forms	aren't	signed

Simple Past Passive

subject	*was/where*	past participle
The machine	was	replaced
The machine	wasn't	replaced
The factories	were	sold
The factories	weren't	sold

The past participle of most verbs is the same as the Simple Past:

e.g. sell   sold   sold

For some verbs, the past participle is different from the Simple Past:

e.g. choose   chose   chosen

See the list of irregular verbs in section 21.

The passive tenses are very often used to talk about process. The person who performs the action is often not mentioned.

e.g. The orders are recorded on this form.
     The documents weren't checked.

If the person who performs the action is mentioned, *by* is used.

e.g. the company was set up **by** John Smith.

6 REPORTED SPEECH

When we report what someone said, we often use *say*. *That* can be left out.

e.g. They **said that** the flight was fully booked.
     They **said** the flight was fully booked.

If the information we report is current, we often do not change the tense of the verb:

We **close** on Sunday. → She said (that) they **close** on
                           Sunday.

If the information we report refers to the past, we change the verb in direct speech from the present to the past.

The hotel **is** full.	→ She said (that) the hotel **was** full.
I **like** the food.	→ She said (that) she **liked** the food.
I'**ll** be home by 8pm.	→ He said (that) he **would be** home by 8pm.
You **can** wait here.	→ She said (that) we **could** wait here.
You **may have to** wait.	→ She said (that) we **might have to** wait.

Notice that the modal verbs *must, could, would, ought* and *might* do not change.

e.g. I **must** call the restaurant.
     She said (that) she **must** call the restaurant.
     I **would** like to visit the factory.
     He said (that) he **would** like to visit the factory.

If the information we report refers to the past, we also change the expression of time:

tomorrow → the next/following day
yesterday → the day before, the previous day

e.g. I'll send them **tomorrow**.
     He said he'd send them **the next day**.

7 THE IMPERATIVE

The imperative form is the same as the infinitive form. We use the same form to talk to one, two or more people. We use *don't* in the negative.

Affirmative:	Negative:
Call me on Monday.	**Don't call** me this evening.
Switch on the printer.	**Don't switch on** the printer.

We use the imperative to:

– make requests

     e.g. **Give** my regards to your boss.
            Don't forget to leave a message.

– offer food and drink

     e.g. **Have** a cup of coffee.
            Try these sandwiches. They're delicious.

– tell someone to do something

     e.g. **Take** the train to Ghent.
            Ask for the Western Industrial Park.

– give orders

     e.g. **Switch off** the lights when you leave.
            Don't leave the lights on.

– give warnings

     e.g. **Be** careful.
            Don't touch that.

8 INFINITIVES AND *-ING* FORMS

We use infinitives with *to*:

– after some verbs (for example, *hope, want, would like, try, need, prefer*)

     e.g. **I hope to see** you again.
            I want to go to the conference.
            I would like to speak to Mr Flock.
            I tried to return your call.
            I need to buy a new suitcase.
            I'd prefer to go to the opera.

– after *something, anything* and *nothing*

     e.g. Would you like **something to drink**?
            Did they have **anything new to say**?

– after some adjectives

     e.g. It's **good to meet** you.
            It's **great to be** here.

– to say why we do things

     e.g. I went to Italy **to visit** some clients.
            Why are you here? **To meet** the new director.

– after *likely*, *unlikely* and *certain*

> e.g. I think sales are **likely to fall**.
> They are **unlikely to increase**.
> They are **certain to fall**.

We use infinitives without *to*:

– after *do* and after modal verbs (*can*, *could*, *may*, *might*, *must*)

> e.g. **Why don't** you **take** a taxi?
> **Could** you **tell** me how to get to the town centre?
> **I might have** a holiday next month.

– after *let's* (*let us*)

> e.g. **Let's have** a break.

– after *would rather*

> e.g. We'**d rather go** on Sunday.

We use *-ing* forms:

– after some verbs (for example, *like*, *love*, *hate*, *prefer*)

> e.g. We **enjoyed having** you here.
> I **like playing** tennis.
> He **loves travelling**.
> I **hate waiting** for people.

– with *need* when it has a passive meaning.

> e.g. I think it ***needs replacing***.
> Does ***it need repairing***?
> It doesn't ***need replacing***.

9 MODAL VERBS

Can, *could*, *may*, *might*, *must*, *have to*, *should*, *ought to* and *would* are called 'modal' verbs. Modal verbs have no *-s* in the third person singular Present.

e.g. She **can** type. (not *She cans type*.)
It **may** rain tomorrow. (not *It mays rain tomorrow*.)

Modal verbs are followed by the infinitive without *to*.

e.g. We **may** be late. (not *We may to be late*.)

Questions and negatives are formed without *do*.

e.g. **Can** you speak Italian? (not *Do you can speak Italian?*)

Note that *cannot* is one word.

Modal verbs have several different meanings and uses.

I can	I cannot (can't)	can I?
you could	you could not (couldn't)	could you?
he, etc. may	she, etc. may not	may it, etc.?
we might	we might not	might we?
you would (you'd)	you would not (wouldn't)	would you?
they must	they must not (mustn't)	must they?

9.1 can *and* could

Can and *could* are used for:

– talking about ability

> e.g. **Can** you make the meeting on Friday?
> I'm sorry, I **can't**.
> **Could** you read my signature?
> Yes, I **could**.

– talking about possibility

> e.g. Business meetings **can** be very boring.
> That **could** be a problem.

– asking for and giving permission

> e.g. **Can** I have the day off?
> You **can** leave early on Friday.

– making requests and offers

> e.g. **Can** I talk to you for a moment?
> **Could** you speak more slowly, please?
> **Can** I help you?

There is little difference between *can* and *could* when used for requests, although *could* is sometimes considered more polite.

9.2 may *and* might

May and *might* are used when:

– talking about possibility

> e.g. I **may** go to the sales conference.
> I **may** not be in the office tomorrow.
> I **might** go on holiday in September.
> I **might** not see you again before you go.

– answering questions which begin with *Do you think …?* and *Will …?*

> e.g. Do you think you'll go to the sales conference? I **may**.
> Will they agree? They **might**.

There is little difference between *may* and *might*, although *might* is sometimes considered a little less sure.

May is used for:

– asking for and giving permission

> e.g. **May** I use your phone?
> Of course you **may**.
> (*Can I use your phone* is less formal and more common.)

9.3 must *and* have to

We use *must* and *have to* for talking about obligation. Often there is no difference in meaning.

e.g. I **have to** call the office. **or** I **must** call the office.
We **have to** pay the bill. **or** We **must** pay the bill.

However, *have to* is usually used when the need comes from the situation <u>outside</u> the speaker.

e.g. I **have to** wear a suit. (It's company policy.)

Must is usually used when the <u>speaker</u> feels something is necessary.

e.g. I **must** go to bed. (I'm tired.)

Must has no Past tense. *Have to* is used to talk about the past.

e.g. They **had to** close the factories.

Must not and *don't have to* mean different things. We use *must not* when there is negative obligation.

e.g. You **mustn't** go to work. (You're ill.)

We use *don't have to* when there is no obligation.

e.g. You **don't have to** go to work. (It's a national holiday.)

Must is also used for:

– inviting

   e.g. You **must** visit us soon. We **must** meet for lunch.

– making deductions

   e.g. You **must** be hungry. They **must** be very busy.

9.4 should *and* ought to

Should and *ought to* are used for giving advice and making suggestions.

e.g. You **should** be in bed.   I think we **should** meet him.
   You **ought not to** smoke.   **Should** I give him a ring.

Should is used for predicting.

e.g. I **should** arrive at three o'clock.
   We **should** be back by then.

9.5 would

Would is used for:

– making offers and requests

   e.g. **Would** you like some more coffee?
      I'**d** like a return ticket to Turin.

– setting up arrangements

   e.g. **Would** Friday be OK?
      Monday **would** be better.

– talking about hypothetical situations

   e.g. I **would** choose Maria.
      The train **would** be cheaper.

10 PHRASAL VERBS

Phrasal verbs are verbs made of two words. Sometimes phrasal verbs have an object. For example:

Verb	Object
try on	a suit
call off	the meeting
switch on	the machine

You can also say:

Try on a suit.	**or**	**Try** a suit **on**.
Call off the meeting.	**or**	**Call** the meeting **off**.
Switch on the machine.	**or**	**Switch** the machine **on**.

But *it, them, me, us* (pronouns) always go <u>before</u> *off, in, on*, etc.

Try it **on**.	**Switch** it **off**.
Plug them **in**.	**Call** it **off**.

11 ARTICLES

11.1 a *and* an

We normally use *an* before a vowel sound – a e i o u:

e.g. **an** engineer, **an** office

We also use *an* before an *h* when it is silent:

e.g. **an** hour

We use *a* before *u/eu* when the sound begins with /j/:

e.g. **a** union, **a** university, **a** European

We normally use *a* before other letters:

e.g. **a** salesman, **a** representative

We use *a* and *an* when we talk about the job we do:

e.g. I'm **a** business manager.
   He's **an** accountant.

We use *a* before common ailments:

e.g. **a** cold, **a** cough

We use no article for most other ailments:

e.g. flu, tonsillitis, arthritis, diabetes

We use *a* and *an* in prices and measurements:

e.g. 80 pence **a** kilo
   50 kilometres **an** hour

Note: In some languages the word for the first number (1) is the same as the article word. This is not so in English. In English, the usual word for *one* is **a** or **an**. *One* is used for special emphasis.

e.g. I'd like **a** coffee and two sandwiches.
   Did you say two sandwiches and two coffees?
   No, two sandwiches and **one** coffee.

11.2 the

We use *the* to talk about particular things which the listener already knows about:

e.g. Did you see **the** advertisement?
   He read **the** proposal.

Department names and job titles can be with or without *the*:

e.g. I'm in **the** accounts department.
I'm in Accounts.
Peter Grant is **the** assistant production manager.
Peter Grant is assistant production manager.

We do not usually use *the* with company names:

e.g. She works for **IBM**.   He has transferred to **Sony**.

But when the name ends with *company* or *corporation*, then *the* is needed:

e.g. He represents **the Sony Corporation**.
The project was financed by **the Triados Bank**.

We do not use *the* when we talk about things in general:

e.g. Business is good.   (not *The business is good.*)
They make cars.   (not *They make the cars.*)

Note these expressions without articles:

e.g. at home (not *at the home*)
go home (not *go to the home*)
at college
at work

12 NOUNS

12.1 *Plurals of nouns*

most nouns simply add -*s*:	manager name	→ managers → names
nouns ending in consonant + -*y*:	secretary company	→ secretaries → companies
nouns ending in -*ch*, -*sh*, -*s* or -*x*:	box address	→ boxes → addresses
some nouns ending in -*f* and -*fe*:	self shelf wife life half knife	→ selves → shelves → wives → lives → halves → knives
some nouns ending in -*f* and -*fe*:	safe cliff roof handkerchief	→ safes → cliffs → roofs → handkerchiefs
most nouns ending in -*o*:	radio photo	→ radios → photos
irregulars:	child man woman potato tomato tooth fish	→ children → men → women → potatoes → tomatoes → teeth → fish

12.2 *Countable and uncountable nouns*

Countable nouns are the names of things that you can count. We can use *a/an* with countable nouns. Countable nouns have plurals.

e.g. a **letter**, one **problem**, two **telephones**,
six hundred **dollars**

Uncountable nouns are the names of things that you can't count. Normally, we can't use *a/an* with uncountable nouns, they have no plurals:

e.g. **milk**, **sugar**, **fruit juice**

Compare:

Countable   – Would you like **a sandwich**?
Uncountable – Would you like **some milk**?   (not *a milk*)
Countable   – There's **a woman** at the reception desk.
Uncountable – There's **some sugar** on the table.

(not *a sugar*)

A/an and *some/any*

We normally only use *a/an* with singular countable nouns. With uncountable nouns, *a/an* is not possible. We can use *some* and *any* with both countable and uncountable nouns (see also section 15).

Countable   – There's **a book** on the desk.
Uncountable – I have **some free time** next week.

(not *a free time*)

Countable   – There are **some books** on the table.
Uncountable – There's **some new information**.

(not *a new information*)

Countable   – Do you have **any stamps**?
Uncountable – Do you have **any news**?

Uncountables

The following words are uncountable. We do not use them with *a/an*, and they have no plurals:

– *advice, information, news, weather, equipment*

e.g. I'd Like to give you **some advice**.   (not *an advice*)
Could you give me **some information**?
(not *an information* or *informations*)
Here is the **news**. (not *a news*)
We're having terrible **weather**. (not *a terrible weather*)
I bought some new **equipment**. (not *a new equipment*)

– *English* (and the names of other languages)

e.g. She speaks very good **English**. (not *a very good English*)

– *medicine, flu, toothache* (but *headache, cold, cough*, etc.
are countable).

e.g. I've got **toothache**.
I've got **flu**.
(but **I've got a headache**.)

Words like *euro, dollar, pound* and *yen* are countable, but the word *money* is uncountable. Some currencies, such as the *yuan* and *rand*, are also countable.

e.g. It cost eight **euros**.
It cost a lot of **money**. (not *a lot of moneys*)
It was 800 **yuan**.

12.3 *Compound word nouns*

Some compound (two-word) nouns are one word.

e.g. bathroom, bedroom, headache

Some compound nouns are hyphenated.

e.g. sitting-room, dining-room

Some compound nouns are written as two words.

e.g. hotel booking, plane ticket, car park

12.4 *Possessive nouns*

We usually use -*s* (singular - '*s*, plural -*s*') for animate/living things.

e.g. Sam is **Mr Veen's** assistant. (not *the assistant of Mr Veen*)
John's surname is Smith.
That is my **boss's** office.
The **directors'** salaries are very high.

Words ending in -*s* usually add - '*s*.

e.g. **Charles's** bag is there.

We usually use *of* for inanimate/not living things.

e.g. The end **of** the week is Friday.
The top **of** the desk is wet.

But there are exceptions. We use - '*s* with days and months.

e.g. Did you read **yesterday's** newspaper?
Last **month's** sales figures were excellent.

For job titles and departments, we can use - '*s* or *of*.

e.g. They are waiting for the **CEO's** arrival.
They're waiting for the arrival **of** the CEO.
The sales **department's** number is 223644.
The number **of** the sales department is 223644.

13 PRONOUNS

13.1 *Subject and object pronouns*

Subject	Object	
I	me	
you	you	e.g. Are **you** Bill Smith? Yes, **I** am.
he	him	Is John from ICT? No, **he** isn't.
she	her	Do you know the managing director?
it	it	Yes, I know **him** very well.
we	us	
you	you	
they	them	

With some verbs, the object pronoun can either go before the verb, or after the verb with *to*.

e.g. Can you **send me** the brochure.
or Can you **send** the brochure to **me**.

13.2 *Possessive adjectives and pronouns*

Adjective	Pronoun	
my	mine	
your	yours	e.g. That's **my** car.
his	his	That car is **mine**.
her	hers	Are they **your** customers?
its	–	They aren't **ours**.
our	ours	
your	yours	
their	theirs	

13.3 *Reflexive/emphatic pronouns*

myself	ourselves
yourself	yourselves
himself	themselves
herself	
itself	

e.g. Did you pack your suitcase **yourself**?
They talked about **themselves**.
I had to make the bed **myself**.

each other

e.g. We write to **each other** once a month. (not *We write to ourselves*)

somebody else

e.g. I didn't write that letter – it was **somebody else**.
Do you usually go on holiday by yourself or with **somebody else**?

13.4 *Relative pronouns*

Who and *that* are used for people.

e.g. The person **who** has the information is away at
the moment.
The man **that** helped me was called Smith.

Which and *that* are used for things.

e.g. The department **which** handles telephone sales is
very busy.
The department **that** I work for is expanding.

We can leave out the relative pronouns *who, which* and *that*
when they are the objects of the relative clause.

e.g. The man (**who/that**) you saw yesterday is the director.

Here, the man is the subject of the main clause (*He is the
director*) and the object of the relative clause (*You saw him*).

e.g. Do you want to see the machine (**which/that**) they
bought?

Here, the machine is the object of the main clause (*Do you
want to see it?*) and the object of the relative clause (*They
bought it*).

14 DEMONSTRATIVES

14.1 this *and* these

This and *these* express nearness to the speaker: near in space,
time and importance. The basic idea is *here* or *in my space*.

e.g. **This** telephone is out of order.
He's arriving **this** afternoon.
These buildings are new.
There are no easy answers to **these** problems.

14.2 that *and* those

That and *those* express distance from the speaker: distance in
space, time and importance. The basic idea is *here* or *not in
my space*.

e.g. Is **that** your boss over there?
That was the worst holiday I've ever had.
Those books in the corner are not mine.
Those points can be discussed later.

14.3 this *and* that *on the telephone*

On the telephone, British people often use *this* to introduce
themselves, and *that* to ask who the person is.

e.g. Hello. **This** is Jane. Is **that** David?

Americans often use *this* is both cases.

e.g. Is **this** David?

15 QUANTIFIERS

15.1 some, any *and* no

We usually use *some* in affirmative ('*yes*') sentences, and
any/no in negative ('*no*') sentences.

Affirmative	Negative
There's **some** coffee.	There isn't **any** coffee.
I've got **some** letters.	I haven't got **any** letters.

In most questions, we use *any*.

e.g. Is there **any** coffee?
Have you got **any** stamps?

We normally use *some* when we offer things.

e.g. Would you like **some** coffee?
Would you like **some** more milk?

We normally use *some* when we ask for things.

e.g. Can I have **some** coffee?
Could you give me **some** paper?

15.2 not any, no *and* none

Note that *not any = no*.

e.g. I'm sorry, there is**n't any** more chicken.
= There's **no** more chicken.
I**'ve** got **no** free time.
= I **haven't** got **any** free time.
(not *I've got any free time*.)

No is used with a noun. *None* is used alone (without a noun).

e.g. There are **no** seats available.
There are **none** at all.

15.3 someone, anybody, everything, nowhere, *etc.*

someone	anyone	everyone	no one
somebody	anybody	everybody	nobody
something	anything	everything	nothing
somewhere	anywhere	everywhere	nowhere

Note that *someone = somebody, anyone = anybody*, etc.

We usually use *some-* in affirmative sentences and *any-* or
no- in negative sentences.

Affirmative	Negative
I want **something** to read.	I don't want **anything** to read.
Someone called for you.	**Nobody** called for you.

Note that *not anyone = no one, not anything = nothing*, etc.

e.g. I did**n't** meet **anyone**. = I met **no one**.
I did**n't** do **anything**. = I did **nothing**.

In questions, both *some-* and *any-* are common.

e.g. Would you like **something** to eat?
Would you like **anything** to eat?
Are you going **somewhere** this evening?
Are you going **anywhere** this evening?

The difference between *some-* and *any-* in these questions is small. *Some-* suggests that you already have a definite idea in mind. *Any-* suggests a totally open question.

Some-, *any-* and *no-* can be followed by adjectives.

e.g. Did you go **somewhere** special?
Did **anything** interesting happen?
Nothing unusual happened.

Every- and *no-* are singular.

e.g. Is **everything** all right?   (not *Are everything all right?*)
Nothing was said.   (not *Nothing ware said.*)
No one is there.   (not *No one are there.*)

Else can be used after all the quantifiers listed above.

e.g. Would you like **anything else**?
It's too busy here. Let's go **somewhere else**.
Nobody else has read the report.

15.4 much, many, a lot of, lots of, a little, a few, enough *and* too

With uncountables	With plurals
(not) much	(not)many
how much?	how many?
too much	too many
a little	a few
a lot of	a lot of
lots of	lots of
enough	enough

e.g. There isn't **much** rain here in the summer.
Are there **many** hotels in the town?

How much time do you need?
How many employees are there in your company?

I've got **too much** work.
You've given me **too many** copies.

These printers make **a lot of** noise.
They've got **lots of** problems.

Have you got **enough** information?
(not *information enough*)
There aren't **enough** car parks in this area.
(not *car parks enough*)

We can also use these words and expressions without nouns.

e.g. **How much** does it cost?
Do you like that restaurant?   **Not much.**
Do you travel **much** for your job?   **A lot.**

We use *much* and *many* mostly in questions and negative sentences. In affirmative sentences, we more often use *a lot* (*of*) or *lots* (*of*).

Compare:
Have you got **many** contacts in Korea?
We haven't got **many** contacts in America.
They've got **a lot of** clients in France.
We've got **lots of** time to get there.

We use *too* (not *too much*) before an adjective or adverb when there is no noun.

Compare:
Am I **too** early? (not *too much early*)
You've got **too much** luggage.

Enough comes after an adverb, and after an adjective if there is no noun.

e.g. You're not speaking **loud enough**. (after adverb)
Is the beer **cold enough** to drink? (after adjective)
We haven't got **enough information**. (before noun)

15.5 both, all, neither *and* one

We can use *both* and *all*:

– with one-part verbs
e.g. We **both read** *The Nation*.   (not *We read both …*)
They **all went** by car.   (not *They went all by car.*)

– with two-part verbs
e.g. We've **both got** appointments.
(not *We both have got …*)
They **will all arrive** tomorrow.   (not *They all will arrive …*)

– with *are* and *were*
e.g. We **are both** available then.
(not *We both are available then.*)
They **were all** in the office.
(not *They all were in the office.*)

both/all/either/neither/one + of + pronoun

e.g. **Both of them** are very busy.
I wish I had time to visit **all of them**.
Either of us could go to the meeting.
Neither of us has seen the samples.
One of us liked the presentation, but the other didn't.

We can also use *both/either/neither/one* without *of* + pronoun.

e.g. Which one do you want?   I'd like **both**.
or   **Both.**
Which one do you want?   I'd like **either**.
or   **Either.**

Both/and and *either/or* can be used to join two ideas.

e.g. The dish comes with (**either**) rice **or** potatoes.
You can (**either**) come with me **or** stay here.
The service was (**both**) quick **and** friendly.
Can you (**both**) telephone **and** send a fax, please.

Note that here *either/both* can be left out.

15.6 another, other *and* others

Another and *other* stand before nouns.

e.g. Have you got **another** one?
     We make two **other** cameras.

Others is only used as a pronoun, referring to other things or other people.

e.g. Can you show me any **others**?
     Have the **others** arrived?

16 QUESTIONS

16.1 *Question words*

Who
Who is calling?
Who's coming this evening?

Whose
Whose coffee is this?
Whose is this coffee?
Whose papers are these?
Whose are these papers?

Which
Which computer would you like to use?
Which of you is responsible for marketing?
(not *Who of you …?*)

What
What is your name? Liz Sanderson.
What does hatchback mean? (not *What means hatchback?*)
What time does the next train leave?
What sort of music do you like?
What do you do? I'm an engineer.
What a nice colour! (not *What nice colour!*)

How
My name is Ann Carter. **How** do you do?
How are you? Very well, thank you. And you?
How old are you? I'm 35.
How did you travel? By car.

Where
Where's the bank? Next to the bookshop.
Where are you from? Barcelona.
Where was this made? Japan.

When
When do you begin your new job? (not *When begins …?*)
When is your next appointment?

Why
Why did you come to London? To learn English.
Why is it more convenient to go by train?

Note that when a question word is the subject of a sentence (or with the subject of a sentence), we form questions without *do*.
Compare:

Who is calling?	(*who* is the subject)
Who did you speak to?	(*who* is the object, *you* is the subject)
What is the address?	(*what* is the subject)
What address do you have?	(*what* is the object, *you* is the subject)
How many people work here?	(*how* is the subject)
How many people do they employ?	(*how* is the object, *they* is the subject)

16.2 *Direct and indirect questions*

Notice the difference in word order between direct and indirect questions.

When **is it?**	(direct)
Do you know when **it is**?	(indirect)
Where **is it?**	(direct)
Can I ask where **it is**?	(indirect)
What time **is the appointment**	(direct)
Can you check what time **the appointment is**?	(indirect)

If there is no question word in the direct question, we use *if* or *whether* in the indirect question.

e.g. Do they sell shoes?   (direct)
     Do you know **if/whether** they sell shoes?   (indirect)

We often use indirect questions to check information.

e.g. Am I right in thinking you**'re arriving on Friday**?
     Can I check that it **starts at 2.15**?

16.3 *Negative questions*

We often use negative questions when we believe that what we are saying is true.

e.g. **Didn't** we order five, not ten?
     Aren't you John Smith?

We also use negative questions in exclamations to show surprise.

e.g. **Isn't** it hot?
     Don't we have any stock?

16.4 *Short answers*

So and *too* are used in answer to affirmative statements. *So* and *too* mean *also*. *So* is used before the verb. *Too* is used after the verb.

Compare:

I work in an office.		**So** do I.
	or	I do **too**.
I have a cold.		**So** do I.
	or	I have one **too**.

Either, *neither* and *nor* are used in answer to negative statements. They mean *also*. *Neither* and *nor* are used before the verb. *Either* is used after the verb.

Compare:

I'm not well.		**Neither** am I.
	or	**Nor** am I.
	or	I'm not **either**.
I've never been to		**Neither** have I.
Mexico City.	or	**Nor** have I.
	or	I haven't **either**.

So can be used after some verbs, e.g. *think, hope, expect, believe* and *I'm afraid*.

e.g. Is she French? I think **so**.
Will Jane be there? I expect **so**.
Has John been invited to the party? I believe **so**.

After all these verbs, we form the negative with *not*. With some of these verbs, we can also form the negative with *so*.

e.g. I **think so.**   I **think not.**   I **don't think so.**
I **hope so.**   I **hope not.**   (not I *don't hope so*.)
I **expect so.**   I **expect not.**   I **don't expect so.**
I **believe so.**   I **believe not.**   I **don't believe so.**
I'm **afraid so.**   I'm **afraid not.**   (not I *don't afraid so*.)

17 ADJECTIVES

17.1 *The form and position of adjectives*

The position of adjectives

Before nouns
e.g. the man in the **blue** suit

After *be*
e.g. the project was **expensive**

The order of adjectives is usually:

opinion	size	age	colour	origin	composition	
a nice	large	new	brown	Italian	leather	bag
a	small	antique		Swiss	gold	watch

The form of adjectives

Adjectives in English have only one form. They have the same form in the singular and plural.

e.g. an **old** building
old buildings

They have the same form with the female and male nouns.

e.g. a **young** woman
a **young** man

17.2 *Comparative and superlative adjectives*

Short adjectives

	Adjective	Comparative	Superlative
most short adjectives:	old young cheap	older younger cheaper	oldest youngest cheapest
adjectives ending in *-e*:	late nice	later nicer	latest nicest
adjectives ending in one vowel + one consonant:	big hot	bigger hotter	biggest hottest
adjectives ending in *-y*:	dry easy	drier easier	driest easiest
irregular:	good bad	better worse	best worst

Longer adjectives

Adjective	Comparative	Superlative
interesting beautiful expensive	more interesting more beautiful more expensive	most interesting most beautiful most expensive

17.3 *Making comparisons*

Comparisons are made:

– with the comparative adjective + *than*

e.g. Monday is **better than** Tuesday for me.
Room 102 is **bigger than** room 202.
The lamb is **more expensive than** chicken.

– with *as* + adjective + *as*

e.g. The meat isn't **as good as** the fish.
Is the salmon **as fresh as** the trout?

Less can be used to form comparatives.

e.g. The old model is cheaper but **less reliable**.

More and *less* can be used with nouns.

e.g. The journey takes **more time** by car.
The journey takes **less time** by train.

17.4 Degrees of comparison

Much, far, a lot, slightly and *a little* can all be used with a comparative adjective.

> e.g. We are **much/far/a lot bigger** than they are.
> We are **slightly/a little smaller** than they are.

Much, far and *slightly* can be used with a comparative adjective and noun.

> e.g. We are a **much bigger** company.
> We are a **far bigger** company.
> We are a **slightly smaller** company.

17.5 Using superlatives

Superlative adjectives are used:

– with *the*

> e.g. It's **the best** one on the market.
> It's **the most reliable**.

– with the possessive

> e.g. It's **our** most expensive product.
> He is **the company's** best salesman.

> Note how we use *least*.

e.g. It's **the least expensive**.
> He's **our least experienced** manager.

By far can be used with superlative adjectives.

e.g. It's **by far the most successful** product.
> It's **by far the least expensive**.

18 ADVERBS

18.1 Adjectives and adverbs

We use adjectives before nouns and after *be*. We use adverbs to give more information about adverbs and adjectives.

Compare:

The company is **efficient**.	(adjective)
They work **efficiently**.	(adverb)
It's **cold**.	(adjective)
It's **extremely** cold.	(adverb)
He was **careful**.	(adjective)
He drove **carefully**.	(adverb)

18.2 Spelling of -ly adverbs

	Adjective	Adverb
most words simply add *-ly*:	slow	slowly
	careful	carefully
	extreme	extremely
adjectives ending in *-y*:	happy	happily
	angry	angrily
adjectives ending in *-able*:	comfortable	comfortably

18.3 Position of adverbs

Don't put adverbs between the verb and the object.

He speaks English **well**.	(not *He speaks well English*.)
He **never** watches TV.	(not *He watches never TV*.)
He read the report **carefully**.	(not *He read carefully the report*.)

18.4 Adverbs of frequency: How often?

> e.g. **How often** do you go to the cinema?
> Do you **ever** go to the opera?

From most to least often:

I **always** have coffee for breakfast.
I **usually** have a bath in the morning.
I **very often** go away at weekends.
I **often** go out in the evenings.
I **sometimes** go to the cinema.
I don't **often** eat fish.
I don't stay at home **very often**.
I **occasionally** travel to France.
I **never** play golf.

Position of frequency:

– with one-part verbs

> e.g. I **always have** coffee for breakfast.
> (not *I have always coffee …*)
> I **very often** go abroad for my work.
> (not *I go very often abroad …*)

– with two-part verbs

> e.g. She **has always been** helpful.
> (not *She always has been …*)
> We **were often invited** to his house.
> (not *We often were invited …*)
> I **can never understand** what she says:
> (not *I never can understand …*)

– with *am/are/is/was/were*

> e.g. She is **usually** late.
> (not *She usually is late*.)
> I **am never** at home these days.
> (not *I never am at home …*)

It is also possible for some adverbs of frequency to be at the beginning of affirmative and negative sentences:

e.g. **Normally**, he won't discuss business.
　　Usually, I don't travel by train.

Regular frequency

I come here	every day.
	every three days.
	once a day.
	twice a week.
	three times a year.

18.5 *Adverbs of degree*

These can be used:

– with adjectives
　e.g. I'm **not at all** hungry.
　　　not very
　　　a bit
　　　quite
　　　very

– with verbs
　e.g. I **very much** like tennis.
　　　I **quite** like golf.
　　　I don't **much** like football.
　　　I don't like basketball **at all**.

18.6 *Adverbs of probability*

Probably, *certainly* and *definitely* take the same positions as adverbs of frequency. (See Section 18.4.)

e.g. You **probably need** the XL 70.
　　You **will certainly need** the XL 70.
　　He **is definitely** in his office.

18.7 *Other adverbs:* far *and* long

We only use *far* and *long* in questions and negative statements.

e.g. How **far** is it to Lublin?　　It isn't **far**.
　　I won't stay **long**.

We normally use *long time*, *long way* and *far away* in positive statements.

e.g. It's a **long way** from here.
　　It will take you a **long time** to drive there.

We can use *long* and *far* after *too*, *so* and *as* in positive statements.

e.g. It's **too far** to drive.
　　The journey took **so long**, I missed the meeting.
　　It takes **as long** by train.

18.8 *Comparative and superlative adverbs*

We usually form comparative and superlative adverbs with *more* and *most*.

e.g. Could you speak **more slowly**?
　　We are operating **more effectively**.

Exceptions: *faster, fastest; better, best; harder, hardest.*
e.g. She can type **faster** than me.
　　I speak English **better** than my colleagues.

19 PREPOSITIONS

19.1 *Talking about time*

in **is used for:**

parts of the day	**in** the morning
months	**in** July
seasons	**in** spring
years	**in** 1985
centuries	**in** the 19th century
how soon something will happen	**in** two days

at **is used for:**

exact times	**at** ten o'clock
holidays and religious festivals	**at** Christmas
night	**at** night
the weekend	**at** the weekend

on **is used for:**

dates	**on** June 22nd
days	**on** Monday
days + *morning, afternoon*, etc.	**on** Friday evening

Other time prepositions:

half **past** nine	five **to** ten
before two o'clock	**after** lunch
until a quarter to three	**from** nine **to/until** six
during the afternoon	**for** two hours
since Christmas	

e.g. I'll see you	**in** three days. (= three days from now)
We will be here	**for** two weeks.
I have been here	**for** six weeks.
	since Easter.
I work	**from** nine **to/until** five.
I'll be here	**until** twenty to three.
I'll be here	**for** two hours.
She will be here	**before** lunch.
I'm free	**after** six o'clock.
It's	half **past** nine.
	five **to** ten.

Approximate time:

I rang you	**at about** three o'clock.
	at around three o'clock.
	just before four.
	not later than six.
I was out	**for most of** the afternoon.

No preposition:

What time do you get up? (not *At what time …?*)
I'm meeting John **tomorrow**.
I'll see you **next week**.
I saw her **last week**.
I was out **all morning**.
She was in meetings **most of the day**.

19.2 *Talking about place*

in	behind	between
on	in front	on the left of
next to	opposite	on the right of

e.g. It's **in** that building.
in the centre.
on the fifth floor.
on an industrial estate.
on the right of the workshop.
next to the canteen.
behind the main entrance.
opposite the kitchen.
between the conference centre and the hotel lobby.

Usually *in* or *at* is possible for a building (*hotel, airport,* etc.).

e.g. We stay **in** a nice hotel.
We stayed **at** a nice hotel.

above	at the top of
below	at the bottom of
at	the end of
by	over there
near	

e.g. It's **above** the canteen.
at the entrance.
below my office.
by the reception desk.
at the top of the stairs.
at the bottom of the stairs.
at the end of the corridor.
near the stairs.

It's **in** his office.
on the second floor.
at no. 53 Park Street.
in Vilnius.
in Lithuania.

He is **at** the station.

at the airport.
at the bus stop.
at the bank.
at home. (not *At the home.*)
at work. (not *At the work.*)
at lunch. (not *At the lunch.*)
on his way to work.

19.3 *Talking about direction*

to	along
down	through
up	past

e.g. Go **to** the end of the corridor.
down those stairs.
up these stairs.
along the main street.
through the car park.
past the bank.

into	down to
onto	back to
up to	out to

e.g. Go **into** the lift.
onto the motorway.
up to the fifth floor.
down to the first floor.
back to the reception desk.
out of the building.

19.4 *Other uses of prepositions*

Here is a letter **for** you.
He's the woman **in** the blue suit.
He works **in** Finance.
Here's the man **with** the beard.
She's **on** the domestic sales side.
What's **on** the menu?
We are all here **except** Johan.
How old is she? **Over** 20.   **Under** 30.
He's good **at** languages.
She's very good **at** tennis.
The highest building **in** the world. (not *… of the world.*)
We went to Turkey **on** holiday.
We went there **by** bus/car/train/air.
I'll think **about** it.
We were talking **about** money.
I can't go **without** sleep for very long.
Look at my office.
Would you like to **listen to** the radio?
I'm **looking for** some new headphones.
I'm phoning **in connection with** the contract.
According to Mr Smith, you have the contract.
I'm **sorry about** the mistake.
Could we meet in London **instead of** Berlin?

20 WORDS TO NOTE

20.1 make *and* let

After *make* and *let*, we use the infinitive without *to*.

e.g. He **made** me write the report again. (not *He made me to write …*)
Could you **let** me have a copy? (not *Could you let me to have a copy?*)

Let's is used to make suggestions.

e.g. **Let's** go now or we will be late.

20.2 make *and* do

Make and *do* are sometimes confused.

Make means to *create* or *construct*:

e.g. We **make** cars. They **make** spare parts.
I'm **making** coffee. Would you like some?
Are you **making** profit?

Make is also used to talk about arrangements:

e.g. Can you **make** five o'clock? No, but I can **make** five-thirty.

Do is used to talk about activities, especially:

e.g. What does your company **do**?
We make components for the car industry.
Who **does** the stationery orders?
David **does**.

Note these other common expressions with *make* and *do*.

e.g. do business   make a suggestion
do the talking   make a decision
do the cooking/washing   make a payment
do my hair   make an appointment
do someone a favour   make arrangements
do better   make a phone call
do worse   make a mistake

20.3 ask, tell *and* say

Ask/tell + object + infinitive form of the verb:

e.g. **Ask** him to call me, please.
Tell John to bring the reports.

Say + (*that*) or *tell* + object + (*that*)

Compare:

Say (that) John Smith phoned.
Tell Alan (that) John Smith phoned.

(*That* can be omitted in these sentences.)

20.4 shall *and* why don't …?

Shall is used to make and to ask for suggestions. It is quite formal. It is used only with *I* and *we*.

e.g. **Shall** I call you tomorrow?
Shall we go through the programme now?
Where **shall** we go?

Why don't/doesn't can also be used for suggestions and is less formal than *shall*.

e.g. **Why don't we** go through the programme now?
Why don't you change the date?
Why doesn't he take a holiday?

20.5 would like *and* want

Would like and *want* are used to make requests and offers. *Would like* is more polite and more common than *want*.

e.g. **I would like** you to do something.
(not *I would like that you do something.*)
Do you **want** me to help you?
(not *Do you want that I help you?*)

20.6 do you mind if …?

Do you mind if …? is used to ask for permission to do something.

e.g. **Do you mind if** I take this call?   Not at all.
No, please do.
Go ahead.

Notice that when you give permission you can begin with a negative (*not, no*). This is because you *don't* mind.

e.g. **Do you mind if** I open the window?
I'd rather you didn't. It's a bit cold.   (not *Yes.*)
Well, actually, I'm rather cold.   (not *Yes, I do.*)
Notice that if you do mind, the simple answer *Yes*, or *Yes, I do* is avoided because it can seem rude or aggressive.

20.7 get

Get is often used in spoken English. It has different meanings:

To get = to receive/buy/fetch/find.

e.g. Did you **get** my email?
Where can I **get** stamps?
Could you **get** my coat for me?
We can't **get** qualified programmers.

To get + cold, hungry, tired, etc. = to become.

e.g. It's **getting** late.
I'm **getting** tired.

To get married = to marry.

e.g. When did he **get** married?
He **got** married last year.

To get to a place = to arrive.

e.g. How did you **get** here?
I usually **get** to work before 9am.

To get + preposition.

e.g. **Get off** the train at Gare du Nord.
He **got out** of the lift on the third floor.
Did you **get on** the plane at Jeddah?
I didn't **get through** all my work yesterday.
Could you **get back** to me?

To get + noun + past participle = to have (as in, *to have something done*).

e.g. Where can I **get** my suit **cleaned**?
Where can I **get** this letter **typed**?

20.8 had better

Had better is similar in meaning to *should*. It can be used to talk about the present and the future.

It is used when action is required.

e.g. We **had better** cancel the booking.

It is used for giving advice.

e.g. You aren't well. You had better stay in bed.
You **had better** not go to work.

20.9 used to

Used to is used for regular actions and events in the past that no longer happen.

e.g. I **used to** play tennis twice a week.

It is also used for past situations that are no longer true.

e.g. I **used to** work in the Milan office.

Note that the negative and interrogative are formed without *-d*.

e.g. Did you **use to** live in Milan?
We didn't **use to** open on Saturdays.

Used to is used with *there* to describe past situations that no longer exist.

e.g. **There used to be** more heavy manufacturing.
There didn't use to be a ferry service.
Did there use to be so much traffic?

20.10 still, yet *and* already

Still is used to talk about things which are happening around now. It is normally:

– before the main verb

e.g. She **still** works for ETP.

– after the verb *to be*

e.g. It's **still** snowing.

– before a negative

e.g. Mr Jones has **still** not answered my letter.

Yet is used to talk about things which we expect. It normally goes at the end of a sentence:

e.g. The taxi hasn't arrived **yet**.
Are you ready? Not **yet**.

Already is used to say that things have happened.

e.g. Mr Smith has *already* left.
I've *already* phoned for a taxi.

20.11 since, in, for *and* ago

Since, for and *in* are used with the Present Perfect tense to talk about things which are still happening or are still important now.

Since is used with a point in time (e.g. six o'clock, Monday, June etc.).

e.g. I've been in this office **since** June.
I haven't been to Bogota **since** 1991.

For is used with a period time (e.g. two days, six months, etc.).

e.g. I've been in this office **for** six months.
I haven't been to Bogota **for** three years.

In can be used with *recent* and *the last* for periods of time related to now.

e.g. Trade has improved **in** recent years.
In the last five years, profits have increased slowly.

Ago is used with the Simple Past tense to talk about things which happened in the past and are finished now. *Ago* is NEVER used with the Present Perfect tense.

e.g. I left school ten years **ago**.
(not *I have left school ten years ago*.)
Stefan joined us three weeks ago.
(not *Stefan has joined us three weeks ago*.)

20.12 for *and* until/till

For is used with a length of time and *until/till* with a point in time. *Till* means exactly the same as *until*.

e.g. I'll be away **for** five days.
I'll be away **until/till** Friday.

20.13 why *and* because

Why is used to ask for a reason. *Because* is used to give a reason.

e.g. Can we change the time of the meeting?
Why? (What's the problem?)
Because the conference room is booked.
(That is the reason.)

20.14 to and in order to

To is often used to talk about why someone does something. *In order to* has the same meaning, but is more formal and/or emphatic.

Compare:

I'm sending it by courier **to** make sure they get it today.
I'm sending it by courier **in order to** make sure they receive it today.

I went to Paris **to** see the new factory.
I'm going to Paris **in order to** see the new factory.

20.15 how and what (a)

In exclamations, we can use *how* before adjectives without nouns. We use *what* (*a*) before adjectives with nouns.

Compare:

How expensive!   **What an** expensive shop!
How generous!   **What a** generous man!
How interesting!   **What** interesting news!

20.16 so and such (a)

We use *so* before adjectives without nouns. We use *such* (*a*) before adjectives with nouns.

Compare:

It's **so** expensive!   It's **such an** expensive shop!
He's **so** generous!   He's **such a** generous man!
The weather is **so** awful!   It's **such awful** weather!
The roads are **so** bad!   They are **such bad** roads!

Notice these examples:

The roads were **so** bad that our journey took three hours.
The ring was **so** expensive that I decided not to buy it.
It was **so** hot last night that I couldn't sleep.
It was **such** terrible weather that we didn't go out.

20.17 one, ones, other and others

One, *ones*, *other* and *others* can be used as substitutes for words already mentioned.

e.g. (This plate is dirty.)
     Here's a clean **one**.
     (Where are the offices?)
     One is in the centre of the city, the **other** is to the west.
     (Have you answered all the letters?)
     No. I answered the urgent **ones**, but I left the **others**.
     It's not easy to choose which **ones** to go for.

20.18 instead of, in place of and instead

Instead of and *in place of* have a similar meaning. Both expressions are followed by a noun.

e.g. I'd like to travel on the four o'clock flight **instead of** the three o'clock one.
     Shall I send you the new model **in place of** the LS 24?

Instead can also be used as an adverb. It is always the last word in a sentence.

e.g. Shall I send you a new model **instead**?
     (not *Shall I send you a new model in place?*)

20.19 only

Only can go in different places in a sentence. When it refers to the subject, it normally goes before it.

e.g. **Only** I know the PIN number.
     Only a few people attended the meeting.

When *only* refers to another part of the sentence, it usually goes in a mid-position.

e.g. He can **only** understand a few phrases in Japanese.
     This shop **only** opens at the weekend.
     I've **only** been to Cairo once.

Sometimes, sentences like this are ambiguous.

e.g. They will **only** ring if the answer is no. (*They won't write.*)
     They will **only** ring if the answer is no. (*They will not ring if the answer is yes.*)

In speaking, we make the meaning clear with intonation. In writing it is best to put *only* directly before the part of the sentence it refers to.

e.g. They will ring **only** if the answer is no.

21 IRREGULAR VERBS

Infinitive	Past tense	Past participle
be	was	been
become	became	become
begin	began	begun
bend	bent	bent
bite	bit	bitten
blow	blew	blown
break	broke	broken
bring	brought	brought
build	built	built
burn	burnt	burnt
buy	bought	bought
can	could/was able	been able
catch	caught	caught
choose	chose	chosen
come	came	come
cost	cost	cost
cut	cut	cut
do	did	done *(cont.)*

Infinitive	Past tense	Past participle
draw	drew	drawn
drink	drank	drunk
drive	drove	driven
eat	ate	eaten
fall	fell	fallen
feed	fed	fed
feel	felt	felt
fight	fought	fought
find	found	found
fly	flew	flown
forecast	forecast	forecast
forget	forgot	forgotten
get	got	got
give	gave	given
go	went	gone
grow	grew	grown
have	had	had
hear	heard	heard
hit	hit	hit
hold	held	held
hurt	hurt	hurt
keep	kept	kept
know	knew	known
lay	laid	laid
lead	led	led
learn	learnt/learned	learnt/learned
leave	left	left
lend	lent	lent
let	let	let
lie	lay	lain
lose	lost	lost
make	made	made
mean	meant	meant
meet	met	met
pay	paid	paid
put	put	put
read	read	read
ride	rode	ridden
ring	rang	rung
rise	rose	risen
run	ran	run
say	said	said
see	saw	seen
sell	sold	sold
send	sent	sent
set	set	set
shake	shook	shaken
shine	shone	shone
show	showed	shown
shut	shut	shut

Infinitive	Past tense	Past participle
sing	sang	sung
sit	sat	sat
sleep	slept	slept
smell	smelt	smelt
speak	spoke	spoken
spell	spelt	spelt
spend	spent	spent
stand	stood	stood
steal	stole	stolen
swim	swam	swum
take	took	taken
teach	taught	taught
tell	told	told
think	thought	thought
throw	threw	thrown
understand	understood	understood
wake up	woke up	woken up
wear	wore	worn
win	won	won
write	wrote	written

22 USEFUL INFORMATION

22.1 *Cardinal numbers*

1	one	19	nineteen
2	two	20	twenty
3	three	21	twenty-one
4	four	22	twenty-two
5	five	23	twenty-three
6	six	24	twenty-four
7	seven	25	twenty-five
8	eight	26	twenty-six
9	nine	27	twenty-seven
10	ten	28	twenty-eight
11	eleven	29	twenty-nine
12	twelve	30	thirty
13	thirteen	40	forty
14	fourteen	50	fifty
15	fifteen	60	sixty
16	sixteen	70	seventy
17	seventeen	80	eighty
18	eighteen	90	ninety

0	oh or zero
12	twelve or a dozen
100	one hundred or a hundred
106	one hundred and six or one hundred six (US)
556	five hundred and fifty-six
1000 or 1,000	one thousand or a thousand
5001 or 5,001	five thousand and one
10 000 or 10,000	ten thousand
1,000,000 or 1m	one million or a million (informal)
1,000,000,000 or 1bn	one billion or a billion (informal)
0.4	point four or nought point four
0.5126	nought point five one two six
$\frac{1}{4}$	one quarter or a quarter (informal)
$\frac{1}{2}$	one half or a half (informal)
$\frac{3}{4}$	three-quarters
$\frac{5}{16}$	five-sixteenths
25%	twenty-five per cent
100%	a hundred per cent
$12\frac{1}{2}$%	twelve and a half per cent
55.5%	fifty-five point five per cent

Notes

1 The point (.) is used to show decimals. The comma (,) is used to show thousands or millions or billions.

2 After the decimal point, you read number by number.

3 The difference between numbers like 13 (thirteen) and 30 (thirty) is sometimes difficult to hear, so it may be necessary to say one-three, three-oh when repeating.

4 British people normally say *and* after hundreds. Americans usually leave *and* out.

5 There is often no comma in 1000.

6 *Hundred*, *thousand*, *million* and *billion* take an *s* when they are used without a number:

e.g. How many boxes are there? Hundreds.
The *s* is dropped when they are used with numbers:

e.g. six billion   twenty thousand
nine hundred   two million

22.2 Ordinal numbers

1st	first	24th	twenty-fourth
2nd	second	25th	twenty-fifth
3rd	third	26th	twenty-sixth
4th	fourth	27th	twenty-seventh
5th	fifth	28th	twenty-eighth
6th	sixth	29th	twenty-ninth
7th	seventh	30th	thirtieth
8th	eighth	40th	fortieth
9th	ninth	50th	fiftieth
10th	tenth	60th	sixtieth
20th	twentieth	70th	seventieth
21st	twenty-first	80th	eightieth
22nd	twenty-second	90th	ninetieth
23rd	twenty-third	100th	hundredth

22.3 Telephone numbers

We say each figure separately. When the same figure comes twice, we can say *double*. *0* is said as *zero* or as *oh*:

e.g. 020 259 366   zero (or *oh*) two zero (or *oh*), two five nine, three six six (or three double six).

22.4 Some telephone alphabets

	American	British	International
A	Able	Andrew	Amsterdam
B	Baker	Benjamin	Baltimore
C	Charlie	Charlie	Casablanca
D	Dog	David	Denmark
E	Easy	Edward	Edison
F	Fox	Frederick	Florida
G	George	George	Gallipoli
H	How	Harry	Havana
I	Item	Isaac	Italy
J	Jig	Jack	Jerusalem
K	King	King	Kilogram
L	Love	Lucy	Liverpool
M	Mike	Mary	Madagascar
N	Nan	Nelly	New York
O	Oboe	Oliver	Oslo
P	Peter	Peter	Paris
Q	Queen	Queenie	Quebec
R	Roger	Robert	Rome
S	Sugar	Sugar	Santiago
T	Tare	Tommy	Tripoli
U	Uncle	Uncle	Uppsala
V	Victor	Victory	Valencia
W	William	William	Washington
X	X-ray	Xmas	Xantippe
Y	Yoke	Yellow	Yokohama
Z	Zebra /ziːbrə/	Zebra /zebrə/	Zurich

22.5 *Ages*

Note the difference in spelling and punctuation.

That man is 30 years old.
He's a 30 year-old man.
The contract is for five years.
It's a five-year contract.

22.6 *Time*

You can ask the time in two ways:

What is (what's) the time? **or** What time is it?

A simple way to tell the time is to say the numbers:

8.15	eight fifteen	9.27	nine twenty-seven
11.30	eleven thirty	7.55	seven fifty-five

You can say the hours in two ways:

nine   nine o'clock

To be exact, you can say:

ten am   ten in the morning
ten pm   ten in the evening

am = midnight to midday   pm = midday to midnight

You can also tell the time in this way:

six o'clock   five past seven   a quarter past eight

half past nine   twenty to ten   a quarter to eleven

2.05 = *Five past two* in British English. *Five after two* in American English.

2.55 = *Five to three* in British English. *Five of three* in American English.

22.7 *Days, months and seasons*

Days	Months	Seasons
Monday	January	spring
Tuesday	February	summer
Wednesday	March	autumn (fall US)
Thursday	April	winter
Friday	May	
Saturday	June	
Sunday	July	
	August	
	September	
	October	
	November	
	December	

Expressions with days, months and seasons:

on Monday	in January	in (the) spring
this Tuesday	next April	last spring
by Saturday	after July	till winter

Festivals

(at) Easter
(at) Christmas
(on) Independence Day

22.8 *Years and dates*

1987 nineteen eighty-seven
1621 sixteen twenty-one
2000 the year two thousand
1905 nineteen five or nineteen hundred and five
       or nineteen oh five

You can ask the date in two ways:

What is (What's) the date? What date is it?

2.1.05	the second of January two thousand and five
or	January the second two thousand and five (In American English, this is the first of February two thousand and five.)
3 June 11	the third of June two thousand and eleven
3 June 1993 **or**	June the third nineteen ninety-three
June 3, 1993 **or**	(American English) June third, nineteen ninety-three
3rd June, 1993	

22.9 *Measurements*

When you describe measurements you say:

    The pipe is five metres long.

or The pipe is five metres in length.

but It is a five-metre pipe.

You can say:

    The cable is two hundred feet long.

but It is a two-hundred-foot cable.

The most common measurements are given in the table below:

Metric	British and American
Length	
1 millimetre	= 0.039 inch
1 centimetre	= 0.3937 inch
1 metre	= 1.094 yards
1 kilometre	= 0.6214 mile
Weight	
100 grammes	= 3.527 ounces
1 kilogramme	= 2.205 pounds
1 tonne	= 0.984 ton
Capacity	
1 decilitre	= 0.176 pints
1 litre	= 1.76 pints
1 decalitre	= 2.20 gallons
Area	
1 square centimetre	= 0.155 sq. inch
1 square metre	= 1.196 sq. yards
1 hectare	= 2.471 acres
1 square kilometre	= 0.386 sq. mile
Volume	
1 cubic centimetre	= 0.061 cu. inch
1 cubic metre	= 1.308 cu. yards

Notes

1 *metre*, *litre*, etc. = *meter*, *liter*, etc. in American English.

2 informal: *kilo*.

3 Some common abbreviations: mm (millimetre), cm (centimetre), m (metre), km (kilometre), ft (foot/feet), g (gramme), kg (kilogramme), oz (ounce), lb (pound), l (litre).

22.10 *Temperature*

Many English-speaking areas, including the US, still give temperatures in Fahrenheit.

To convert Fahrenheit to Centigrade, subtract 32 and multiply by $\frac{5}{9}$.

To convert Centigrade to Fahrenheit, multiply by $\frac{9}{5}$ then add 32.

Centigrade is also called *Celsius*.

Fahrenheit

Water freezes at thirty-two degrees Fahrenheit (32^0F).

Last night we had ten degrees of frost (22^0F).

It was ninety-five in the shade this morning (95^0F).

Centigrade

Water freezes at nought degrees Centigrade (0^0C).

Last night, the temperature was ten degrees below zero (-10^0C).

It was thirty-five in the shade this morning (35^0C).

22.11 *Money*

British

You write:	You say:
1p	one penny
	or one pence
	or one p
56p or 0.56	fifty-six pence
	or fifty-six p
£1	one pound
	or a pound
£1.20	one pound twenty
	or one pound twenty pence
£3.75	three pounds seventy-five
	or three pounds (and) seventy-five pence
£5m	five million pounds
£5.5	five point five million pounds
	or five and a half million pounds
	or five million, five hundred thousand pounds

American

You write:	You say:
1c or $0.01	one cent
56c	fifty-six cents
$1	a dollar
	or one dollar
$1.20	one dollar twenty
	or one dollar and twenty cents
$3.75	three dollars seventy-five
	or three dollars and seventy-five cents
$3bn	three billion dollars

22.12 *Countries and nationalities*

To talk about people and things from a particular country, you have to know three words:

– the adjective used to refer to the country

– the word used for a person from the country

– the word used (with *the*) to refer to the whole nation.

Usually the word used for a person is the same as the adjective. The word used for the nation is the plural of this. However, in some cases there is a different form for the person. Apologies to countries not included in the list that follows.

Country	Adjective	Person	Nation
Albania	Albanian	an Albanian	the Albanians
Algeria	Algerian	an Algerian	the Algerians
America	American	an American	the Americans
Argentina	Argentinian	an Argentinian	the Argentinians
Australia	Australian	an Australian	the Australians
Austria	Austrian	an Austrian	the Austrians
Belgium	Belgian	a Belgian	the Belgians
Brazil	Brazilian	a Brazilian	the Brazilians
Britain	British	a Briton	the British
Bulgaria	Bulgarian	a Bulgarian	the Bulgarians
Canada	Canadian	a Canadian	the Canadians
China	Chinese	a Chinese	the Chinese
Czech Republic	Czech	a Czech	the Czechs
Denmark	Danish	a Dane	the Danes
Egypt	Egyptian	an Egyptian	the Egyptians
England	English	an Englishman	the English
Finland	Finnish	a Finn	the Finns
France	French	a Frenchman	the French
Germany	German	a German	the Germans
Greece	Greek	a Greek	the Greeks
Holland	Dutch	a Dutchman	the Dutch
Hungary	Hungarian	a Hungarian	the Hungarians
India	Indian	an Indian	the Indians
Iran	Iranian	an Iranian	the Iranians
Ireland	Irish	an Irishman	the Irish
Italy	Italian	an Italian	the Italians
Japan	Japanese	a Japanese	the Japanese
Kenya	Kenyan	a Kenyan	the Kenyans
Korea	Korean	a Korean	the Koreans
Lebanon	Lebanese	a Lebanese	the Lebanese
Libya	Libyan	a Libyan	the Libyans
Malaysia	Malaysian	a Malaysian	the Malaysians
Mexico	Mexican	a Mexican	the Mexicans
Norway	Norwegian	a Norwegian	the Norwegians
Poland	Polish	a Pole	the Poles
Oman	Omani	an Omani	the Omanis
Russia	Russian	a Russian	the Russians
Scotland	Scottish	a Scot	the Scottish
Slovakia	Slovak	a Slovak	the Slovaks
Spain	Spanish	a Spaniard	the Spanish
Sweden	Swedish	a Swede	the Swedes
Ukraine	Ukrainian	a Ukrainian	the Ukrainians
Uruguay	Uruguayan	a Uruguayan	the Uruguayans

22.13 Geographical location

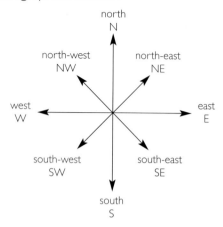

e.g. Where is your head office?
80 kilometres west of Cairo.

Do you have any distribution centres in Egypt?
Yes, in the south-west of the country.

22.14 Parts of the world

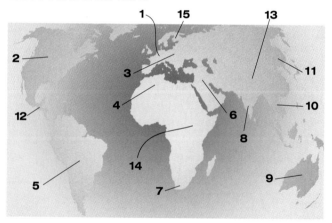

1 Western Europe
2 North America
3 Eastern Europe
4 North Africa
5 South America
6 Middle East
7 Southern Africa
8 India/South Asia
9 Australia
10 South-East Asia
11 Far East/Asia Pacific
12 Central America
13 Central Asia
14 East Africa
15 Scandinavia

The names for different regions of the world can vary depending on where you live.

22.15 *Titles*

Mr is used for married and unmarried men.
Miss is used for unmarried women.
Mrs is used for married women.
Ms is used for married and unmarried women.

Notes

1 *Mr* (= *Mister*) is not usually written in full. The other titles cannot be written in full.

2 *Dear Sir* and *Dear Madam* are ways of beginning letters to people you don't know. In other situations, *Sir* and *Madam* are unusual.

   e.g. Excuse me, could you tell me the time?
   (not *Excuse me, sir.*)

22.16 *Abbreviations*

There are many abbreviations. Some are widely used. Some are used only within one industry, company or even a department of a company. The list that follows includes only some of the abbreviations used in this book. They are all widely used. (See Section 22.9 for abbreviated measurements.)

admin.	administration
CEO	chief executive officer
CFO	chief financial officer
Co.	company
dept	department
e.g.	for example
etc.	*etcetera* (Latin) = and so on
HQ	headquarters
Inc.	incorporated (after names of business organisations; the American equivalent of Ltd)
IT	information technology
km/l	kilometres to the litre
Ltd	limited (after names of private limited companies)
MD	managing director
NB	*nota bene* (Latin) = note well
PA	personal assistant
pda	personal digital assistant (e.g. a 'palm' handheld computer)
PIN	personal identification number
PLC	public limited company
PTO	please turn over
R&D	research and development
rep	representative
VAT	value-added tax

22.17 *British and American English*

Some differences in spelling:

British	American
cancelled	canceled
centre	center
dialled	dialed
litre	liter
metre	meter
theatre	theater
through	thru
travelled	traveled

22.18 *Notes on verb contractions*

In speech and in formal writing, some verb forms are contracted with:

- personal pronouns: *I'm* (I am), *they've* (they have), etc.
- question words: *What's* (What is), *How'll* (How will), etc.
- demonstrative pronouns: *that's* (that is), *these're* (these are), etc.
- there: *there's* (there is), *there'd be* (there would be), etc.

Contracted forms are not used in affirmative short answers:
Yes, I am. (not *Yes, I'm.*)
Yes, they have. (not *Yes, they've.*)

However, they are used in negative short answers:
No, we don't.
No, she can't.

The following contracted forms are used in this book:

is/are
I'm (I am), *he/she/it's* (he/she/it is), *there's* (there is), *What's* (What is), *Where's* (Where is), *that's* (that is), *these're* (these are), *isn't* (is not), *we/you/they're* (we/you/they are), *there're* (there are), *aren't* (are not)

was/were
wasn't (was not), *weren't* (were not)

has/have
he/she/it's (he/she/it has), *I/we/you/they've* (I/we/you/they have), *hasn't* (has not), *haven't* (have not)

do/did
don't (do not), *didn't* (did not)

will/can
I/you/he'll (I/you/he will), *won't* (will not), *can't* (cannot)

would/must/could/should
I/we/you/she'd (I/we/you/she would), *wouldn't* (would not), *couldn't* (could not), *shouldn't* (should not)

Glossary of business-related terms

accountant: 1 person who keeps a company's accounts
  2 person who advises a company on its finances
accounts: 1 record of transactions over a period of time
  2 department in a company which deals with money paid, received, borrowed or owed
admin: administration
administration: organisation or control or management of a company, e.g. sales administration
advertising: business of announcing that something is for sale or of trying to persuade customers to buy a product or service, e.g. advertising department
advice note: written notice to a customer giving details of goods ordered and shipped but not yet delivered
air freight: transport by airplane
assembly plant: factory where cars are put together from parts made in other factories
asset: thing which belongs to a company or person, and which has a value
associate: 1 connected in some way, e.g. an associate company, 'XYZ Associates'
  2 person who works in the same business as someone, e.g. a business associate
audit: examination of the books and accounts of a company
auditor: company or person who audits the books and accounts, usually an external firm of accountants
balance: amount remaining, e.g. *I'll pay the balance next week. The balance of the order = the rest of the order.*
balance sheet: statement of the financial position of a company at a particular time
bank transfer: moving money from one bank account to another account
board: group of people who run an organisation, e.g. the board of directors of a company
board of directors: group of directors elected by the shareholders to run a company
bookkeeper: person who keeps the financial records of a business
booming: expanding or becoming prosperous, e.g. business is booming
branch: local office of a bank or large business
brewery: the place where beer is made
brochure: publicity booklet
budget: plan of expected spending and income
capital expenditure: money spent on fixed assets (property, machines, furniture)

card: business card showing a person's name and the company he/she works for
carrier: company which transports goods
catering department: the department which provides food
CEO: chief executive officer
CFO: chief financial officer
chain: a number of stores belonging to the same company, e.g. a chain of shoe shops, a hotel chain
Chamber of Commerce: group of local business people who meet to discuss problems which they have in common and to promote commerce in their town/area
chief: most important, e.g. chief accountant
chief executive officer: executive in charge of a company
CIF or c.i.f.: cost, insurance and freight (an export price that is given CIF includes the cost of transportation and insurance to the port of destination)
client: person or company with whom you do business or who pays for a service
club class: a class of airline ticket between first class and tourist
Co.: company
colleague: person who works with you
commerce: business, the buying and selling of goods and services ('commercial' means related to business, e.g. commercial premises)
commission: money paid to a sales person or company, usually a percentage of the value of sales made
computer software: computer programmes (as opposed to computer hardware/machines)
consignment: 1 (informal use) a quantity of goods sent or to be sent
  2 (technical use) goods sent to someone who then sells them for you in return for commission
construction company: company which specialises in building
consultant: specialist who gives advice
contact: person you know or person you can ask for help or advice
container: very large metal case for loading and transporting goods in trucks, trains and ships
contract: legal agreement between two parties
controller: person who controls, especially the finances of a company, e.g. financial controller
coordinator: person who organises the people and things involved in an activity, e.g. sales coordinator

corporate hospitality: entertainment of important clients, usually by senior management

corporation: large company

cost-effective: producing the best results in relation to the cost incurred

costing: calculation of the costs and therefore the selling price of a product or service

courier: person or company that arranges to take parcels or messages from one place to another

credentials: written evidence giving proof of identity or authority

credit card: plastic card which allows you to borrow money and to buy goods without paying for them immediately – you pay the credit card company (e.g. Diners, Visa, Amex) later

credit control: checking that customers pay on time and do not owe more than their credit limit (credit controller is a person who checks payment and contacts customers when it is late)

credit note: note given to someone showing that an amount of money is owed to them

creditor: person or company to whom money is owed

customer service: department which deals with customers and their queries/complaints

Customs and Excise: UK government department which organises the collection of taxes on imports

data processing: analysing data stored in a computer in order to produce management information

degree: qualification obtained from a university, e.g. a degree in business studies

delegate: person who represents others at a meeting or conference

department: specialised section of a large company, e.g. sales department, department secretary

depot: central warehouse for goods, e.g. distribution depot

depressed: reduced; a 'depressed market' is one in which there are more goods than customers

deputy: person who can take the place of another, e.g. the deputy manager

despatch: send goods to a customer

devaluation: reduction in value of a currency against other currencies

director: senior person who is in charge of a division or department, e.g. Personnel Director, Finance Director; senior directors are appointed by the shareholders

discount: percentage by which a full price is reduced (to a buyer) by the seller; 'volume discount' is a discount given to a customer who buys a large quantity of goods

distribution: sending goods from the manufacturer to the wholesaler and then to retailers

distribution network: system for distributing products

domestic: home, e.g. domestic market, domestic sales

door to door: 1 direct from one place to another **2** going from one house to the next, asking the occupiers to buy something or vote for someone

draft: first rough plan, e.g. draft schedule

E&OE: errors and omissions excepted (printed on an invoice to show that mistakes can be corrected at a later date)

effluent: waste matter

email: electronic mail, sending messages from one computer terminal to another via telephone lines

engineer: person who looks after technical equipment, e.g. electrical engineer

estimate: calculation of probable cost or size or time of something

executive: usually a manager or director of a company who makes decisions (NB a 'sales executive' is a sales rep)

export: to sell goods to buyers in foreign countries

ex works: way of quoting a price which does not include transport from the factory; the price at the factory gate

factory floor: internal area of a factory where the manufacturing work is done

finance department: department which deals with the money used by a company

financial services: offering advice and financial products to consumers, e.g. pensions, savings plans

financial statement: document which shows the financial situation of a company

financial year: period, usually twelve months, used by companies for tax and accounting purposes

fleet of (lorries): a number of

flexitime: system where workers can start or stop work at different hours provided that they work a certain number of hours per day or week

FOB or f.o.b.: free on board (price including all seller's costs until goods are on ship for transportation)

forwarder: person or company which arranges shipment of goods to their destination

forwarding agent (forwarder): company that arranges shipping/transportation and customs documents for goods

fund: money set aside for a special purpose; a 'fund management company' is a company that deals with the investment of sums of money on behalf of clients

GNP: a gross national product (value of goods and services produced in a country in a year, including income from other countries)

goods: products

gross figure: total figure with no deductions

group: several companies linked together in the same organisation, e.g. the group headquarters

guarantee: legal document which promises that, e.g., a machine will work properly or that an item is of good quality

hangar: a large building/shed in which aircraft are kept

haulage company: company which transports goods by road

haulier: haulage company or person involved in the haulage business

head office: main office, where the board of directors works and meets

headed notepaper: notepaper with the name and address of a company printed on it

heavy manufacturing: making of large products, e.g. steel bars, ships, railway engineers

hi-tech industries: industries using the most modern and sophisticated technology

home: in the country where a company is based, e.g. home market, home sales

hospitality company: a company that arranges hospitality for corporate clients (companies)

HR: Human Resources

human resources department: personnel department

import: goods bought from foreign suppliers and brought into a country

Inc (US): incorporated

industrial estate: area specifically reserved for factories and warehouses

industrial park: industrial estate

industrial relations: relations between management and workers

insurance broker: person who arranges insurance for clients

interim: coming before the final version, e.g. interim results, interim payments

invest: 1 spend money on something which you believe will be useful, e.g. to invest money in new machinery, to invest in a factory
2 put money into shares, bonds etc. in the hope that it will produce interest and increase in value

investment: 1 purchase of machines, materials etc. in order to make goods to sell
2 placing of money so that it will produce interest and increase in value

invoice: (noun) note asking for payment for goods or services supplied
(verb) to send an invoice to someone

IT: information technology

itinerary: list of places to be visited on a journey or trip

labour: workforce

laptop computer: portable personal computer

lease: to let or rent land, offices or machinery for a period of time

ledger: book or system in which accounts are kept

liaison officer: person responsible for communication and contact between organisations

limited company: company where members/shareholders are responsible for the debts only up to the value of the shares they hold

load: (noun) a volume of goods that are transported, e.g. a lorry load, a container load
(verb) to put goods into a transporter, e.g. to load a ship, to load goods onto a plane

loan: something which has been lent, usually money, e.g. bank loan

logistics management: controlling the movement of goods; note also 'supply chain management'

Ltd: limited, e.g. Joe Smith Ltd (see **limited company**)

machine hall: part of a factory where machines operate

mail order: system of buying and selling from a catalogue and delivering by mail

maintenance: keeping things going or working, e.g. maintenance department, maintenance engineer

management information system: equipment and procedures which provide managers with information, usually computerised

manager: head of a department in a company, e.g. transport manager, regional manager

managing director: director who is in charge of a whole company

manufacturer: person or company which produces machine-made products

margin: difference between the cost of a product and the money received with selling it, e.g. profit margin

market: area where a product might be sold, or group of people who might buy a product

marketing department: department in a company which specialises in using marketing techniques (e.g. packaging, advertising) to sell a product

MD: managing director

merchandise: goods which are for sale or have been sold

merchant: person who buys and sells goods in bulk for re-sale

merger: joining together of two or more companies

multinational (company): company which has branches or subsidiary companies in several countries

multiple retailer: chain of stores belonging to the same company

negotiable: 1 can be exchanged for cash, goods etc.
2 can be changed or agreed by discussion

net: price or weight or pay etc. after all deductions have been made

network: system that links different points together, e.g. a distribution network

office manager: person responsible for the administration of an office or group of offices

office services: variety of services offered to an office, e.g. cleaning and maintenance, office equipment, service and repair

officer: title sometimes given to a person with an official position in a company, e.g. liaison officer

OHP: overhead projector

open plan office: large room divided into smaller working spaces with no fixed divisions between them

operation: business organisation and work, e.g. a company's operation in Eastern Europe

organisation chart: chart showing the way a company is organised, the names of the departments and the senior management

outlet: place where something can be sold

overdraft: money in excess of the amount in their account which a person or company can withdraw with the permission of the bank

overheads: costs not directly related to producing goods/services, e.g. directors' salaries

PA: personal assistant

packaging: materials used to protect goods which are being packed

pallet: flat wooden base on which goods can be stacked for easy handling by a forklift truck

paperwork: office work, especially writing memos and filling in forms

parent company: company which owns and controls a smaller company

partnership: unregistered business where two or more people (but not more than 20) share the risks and profits according to a partnership agreement

payroll: 1 list of people employed and paid by a company **2** money paid by a company in salaries

pension fund: money which provides pensions for retired members of staff

permanent staff: employees with a permanent contract, as opposed to temporary staff

personal assistant: secretary who works for one particular person

personnel: the people employed in an organisation

personnel department: section of a company which deals with staff matters (see also **human resources**)

plant: factory

PLC: public limited company

power station: place where electricity is generated

pp: *per procreationem* (Latin); to pp a letter is to sign on behalf of someone else

PR: public relations

premises: building and the land it stands on

private sector: all companies which are owned by private shareholders, not by the state

processing plant: factory where raw materials are changed into products by the use of machinery

product: thing which is made or manufactured

production: making or manufacturing goods for sale

production planner: person who plans a production schedule

profile: brief description

profit and loss statement: statement of a company's expenditure and income over a period of time (almost always one calendar year) showing whether a company has made a profit or loss

progress report: report on how work is going

projected: planned or expected, e.g. projected figures

public limited company: company in which the general public can invest, and whose shares are bought and sold on the Stock Exchange

public relations: keeping good relations between a company and the general public

publicity material: sheets or posters or leaflets used to attract the attention of the public to products or services

purchaser: person or company which buys/purchases

purchasing department: department responsible for buying/purchasing

quality assurance: ensuring/checking that goods are of a certain standard

quote: quotation, an estimate of how much something will cost

R&D: Research and Development

rail freight: transport by rail/train

range: series of items from which the customer can choose, e.g. *We offer a wide range of sizes*

rationalisation: process of streamlining or making more efficient

reception: place (in a hotel or office) where visitors register or say who they have come to see

recession: fall in trade or the economy

reclaim: claim back, e.g. reclaim travel expenses

recruitment agency: agency responsible for finding new staff for a company

redevelopment: rebuilding and/or modernising structures or facilities, e.g. factories, road systems

redundant: no longer employed, because the job is no longer necessary

refinery: factory where raw materials are processed to remove impurities, e.g. oil refinery, sugar refinery

refund: money paid back, e.g. for returned goods

registration number: official number, e.g. car registration number

remittance: money sent as payment for something

rep: representative, e.g. sales rep

representative: person or company which acts on another's behalf showing or selling goods or services

Research and Development department: department which carries out scientific investigation leading to new products or improvement of existing ones

retail: sale of general goods to the public, e.g. retail dealer, retail outlet

run: manage or organise

sales: 1 money received for selling something **2** number of items sold

sales conference: meeting of sales managers, representatives, publicity staff etc., to discuss results and future sales plans

schedule: timetable or plan made in advance

security: 1 staff who protect an office or factory, e.g. from burglars
2 system which protects, e.g. electronic security system

senior: older or more important, e.g. senior administrative manager

serial number: number in a series, used to identify a product

share: official document showing that the holder shares ownership of a company; shares usually entitle the holder to receive a dividend (share of the profits) and to vote at the AGM (Annual General Meeting)

shareholder: person who owns shares in a company

shift system: a system where one group of workers work for a period and are then replaced by another group

shipment: goods sent

shipping agent: company which specialises in the sending of goods

site: place or location, e.g. building site, factory site, site plan

skilled: having learnt certain skills, e.g. skilled worker

statement: detailed list; a 'financial statement' is a statement about financial position; a 'statement of expenses' is a detailed list of money spent

Stock Exchange: place where shares in public companies can be bought and sold

stocktaking: counting of goods in stock at the end of an accounting period

storage: keeping in a store or in a warehouse

store: storeroom, place where goods are kept

subcontract: to agree with a company that it will do part of the work for a project

subcontractor: a company which is subcontracted to do the work

subsidiary: company which is owned by a parent company

supervisor: person who organises work and checks that it is well done, e.g. production supervisor

supplier: person or company which supplies or sells goods or services

switchboard: central point in a telephone system, where all lines meet

systems analysis: person who specialises in systems analysis

takeover: buying a controlling interest in a business by buying more than 50% of its shares

target: goal to aim for, e.g. sales target

technician: person with technical expertise, e.g. electrical technician, laboratory technician

telecommunications: systems of passing messages over long distances, e.g. by cable, radio or satellite

telesales: sales made by telephone

terms and conditions: conditions which have to be carried out as part of a contract, or arrangements which have to be agreed before a contract is valid

trade: wholesale, e.g. trade price, trade discount

trainee: person who is learning how to do something

turnover: total sales of a company including goods and services

union: organisation which represents it members in discussions with management, e.g. over wages and conditions of work

unit: single building or small department, e.g. medical unit, translation unit

upgrade: to increase the importance or quality of something, e.g. to upgrade a person's job, to upgrade from tourist to business class

van: small vehicle used for carrying goods

VAT: value-added tax

vice president (US)**:** one of the executive directors of a company

videophone: telephone which allows callers to see one another on a screen

voicemail: telephone system with recorded instructions to the user, which allows him/her to send or receive messages to be retrieved at a later time

voucher: paper which is given instead of money, e.g. lunch voucher

warehouse: large building where goods are stored

warranty: a document which promises that an item will be repaired or replaced within a certain period if it no longer works

wholesale: buying goods in bulk from manufacturers and selling to retailers

work in progress: goods which are partly manufactured or unfinished

workforce: all the workers in an office or factory

works: factory, e.g. glass works, works manager

workshop: 1 small factory
2 area in a building where mechanical work is done

Answers

UNIT 1 You and your background

1 **a** iv   **b** iii
   c i   **d** ii

2 **a** for   **b** in
   c for   **d** with
   e for   **f** in
   g to   **h** to
   i of   **j** from
   k in

3 **a** single, married, separated
   b mother-in-law, brother-in-law, father-in-law
   c golf, football, tennis
   d school, college, university
   e administration, data processing, production
   f degree, certificate, diploma
   g accountancy, engineering, law

4 (possible answers)
   a I work for a company called MAX – it's a hotel group.
   b I'm in the admin department – I'm responsible for coordinating our plans for new hotels.
   c I work in our head office in Brussels.
   d I usually go by bus.
   e I come from Auckland in New Zealand.
   f I live in Brussels, in the suburbs.
   g I like being in Europe and working in Brussels very much.

   (possible paragraph)
   I work for the MAX hotel group. I'm in the admin department – I'm the planning manager. I'm responsible for coordinating our plans for new hotels. I work in our head office in Brussels. I usually go to work by bus – I live in the suburbs. I'm from Cape Town in South Africa. I like being in Europe and working in Brussels very much. I'm here with my wife and my son, Jamie, who is four. In my spare time I watch TV or we go out with friends. Yes, I like travelling abroad – this is lucky because I have to travel a lot in my job.

5 **a** With the Telco group
   b HR manager
   c 28
   d He is a systems analyst with Kettle and Forbes.
   e The payroll and management information systems.
   f She has a degree in business and communications.

UNIT 2 Company structure

1 **a** ii   **b** iv
   c i   **d** iii

2 **a** –   **b** the
   c the   **d** –
   e an   **f** –
   g –, –, –   **h** a
   i an   **j** the, the

3 (possible answers)
   a is responsible
   b Joe Roger
   c R&D (Research and Development)
   d Under
   e Joe Roger (the Production Director)
   f Marc Vicario is responsible for purchasing.
   g Rex Took is in charge of sales and marketing.
   h Cindy Smith reports to Lars Norman.

4 (sample answers)
   a I work for Quicklang Ltd.
   b It's a language training business.
   c It's a limited company.
   d No, we aren't.
   e Helmut Handel. He is the director.
   f It's in Hamburg. We're based there.
   g I'm in the administration department. I do.
   h Ten full time staff and three part time.

5 **a** Dutch   **b** French
   c German   **d** Belgian
   e Hungarian   **f** Polish
   g Brazilian   **h** Japanese
   i Scottish   **j** Chinese

UNIT 3 Company history

1 (possible answers)
   1982: The speaker's uncle bought the factory.
   1983: The speaker and his family moved to America.
   1986: The company merged with US Leather and the head office was moved to Chicago.
   1995: The merged company employed over 2,000 people.
   1997: The speaker was sent to Europe to open a European sales office.
   2004: The company was taken over and the speaker lost his job.
   Now: He's working for PLT Logistics, on the sales side.

2 **a** caught   **b** wore
   c bought   **d** spent
   e wrote   **f** got

3 a merger **b** acquisition
c takeover **d** expansion
e decrease

Note: closed down = closed; taken over = bought by another company

4 a at...on **b** at
c at **d** in
e in **f** in

Note: was set up = was founded, established

5 a A factory was bought in the States in 1997.
b Our Japanese subsidiary was acquired in 1999.
c It was closed in 2004.
d We were taken over by ZRF in 2005.
e The original factory was pulled down.

UNIT 4 Current projects

1 a COUNTRY: Norway
START-UP: August
b COUNTRY: Scotland
SCHEDULE: Two months behind schedule
START-UP: Next spring
c COUNTRY: China
SCHEDULE: On schedule
START-UP: On target for completion in January

2 a I am writing **b** going well
c ahead of **d** the end of next week
e is going **f** working on
g skilled **h** I think

3 a How is it going?
b Do you speak German? / Are you speaking German?
c What are they working on at the moment?
d We build a lot of warehouses like this. / We are building a lot of warehouses like this.
e I don't know your email address.
f I don't think we will finish on schedule.

g We want to start work on the project next month.

4 a in/at **b** on
c at **d** at
e with **f** on/at

5 a The packaging business.
b They sell a range of packaging materials.
c In Northern Europe.
d A big order for FTZ, a Norwegian company.
e They are trying to increase their sales in the American market.
f She is working on some samples for a customer in Detroit.

A paragraph (possible answer)
I am trying to study English on my own. There is a teacher at work but I cannot go to the classes because they are in the evening and I have to get home – we have a young baby. I try to study a little every day but it's difficult. At the moment, my English is getting worse because I'm not studying enough.

UNIT 5 Meeting a visitor

1 a Excuse me.
b How do you do?
c Pleased to meet you.
d Welcome to
e That's very kind of you.
f It wasn't too bad.
g The plane was on time?
h Whose is this carrier bag?
i That belongs to me too.

2 a meet **b** flight
c take **d** booked
e hope **f** confirm
g satisfactory **h** seeing
i Regards

3 (possible answers)
a – Whose is this briefcase? / Whose briefcase is this?
– I think it belongs to Lu.
b – Who do these keys belong to?
– They're Mary's.

c – Whose is this mobile phone? / Whose mobile phone is this?
– I don't know, it isn't mine.
d – Who does this laptop belong to?
– It's Dmitry's.
e – Whose are these papers? / Whose papers are these?
– I don't know, they don't belong to us.
f – Who do these glasses belong to?
– Aren't they yours?
g – Who does this security pass belong to?
– It's Arabella's.
h – Whose are these gloves? / Whose gloves are these?
– They belong to me.

4 a [1] And this is mine too.
b [2] And this is her luggage too.
c [1] And this is ours too.
d [3] And this belongs to him too.
e [3] And these belong to me too.
f [1] And this is hers too.
g [3] And these belong to us too.
h [1] And these are yours too.

5 (possible answers)
a The food was delicious, but the service was poor.
b It was a useful trip, but the weather wasn't good.
c The hotel was comfortable, but the staff on reception weren't helpful.
d The queue for check-in was slow, but passport control was quick.
e Their facilities were excellent, but their prices were high.

UNIT 6 Introducing your home town

1 a hotel
b exhibition centre
c successful
d town hall
e railway station
f Eastern Europe
g 1.2 million

2
  a four hundred and seven thousand
  b three hundred
  c two thousand one hundred
  d one thousand and ninety-nine
  e one thousand one hundred and five
  f one hundred and forty-three thousand two hundred and eighty
  g one hundred and forty-seven million
  h eleven and three-quarter million

3 (possible answers)
  a This   **b** these
  c that   **d** those
  e this   **f** this
  g that   **h** that
  i those   **j** that

4
  a aren't...were/used to be
  b was/used to be
  c is...was/used to be

5 (possible questions)
  a What is the population of Haranga?
  b What are the main industries?
  c Is there a lot of heavy manufacturing?
  d What are the road and rail links like?
  e How far is it to the nearest airport?
  f Is there a cathedral in Haranga?
  g When did the zoo close?
  h How many cinemas are there in Haranga?

UNIT 7 Chance meetings

1 a ii   **b** iii
  c i

2 a ii   **b** vi
  c i   **d** v
  e iv

3 (possible answers)
  a give   **b** Please say
  c Tell/Get   **d** Let
  e What   **f** What
  g How

4 a Good   **b** these days
  c still   **d** on business
  e must

5 a I've just seen John.
  b They've gone.
  c You've just missed him.
  d How long have you been married?

UNIT 8 Shopping

1 a Can I help you?
  b Can you tell me what size you are?
  c How much are they?
  d How much is that in dollars?
  e Have you got anything cheaper?
  f What about these?
  g Can I try them on?

2 a large, extra large, medium, small
  b cotton, wool, nylon, polyester
  c waist, collar, sleeve, chest
  d socks, gloves, tights, trousers
  e chocolates, flowers, jewellery, perfume
  f chemist, supermarket, newsagent, shoe shop

  Notes: jewellery (UK spelling) = jewelry (US spelling)

3 a They don't make clothes big enough.
  b It's too small for me.
  c These shoes are too tight for me.
  d We don't have enough time.
  e I'm too busy to do it now.

4 (possible answers)
  a Do you know what colour you want?
  b Can you tell me if you have a bigger one?
  c Do you know if you have anything cheaper?
  d I need to know if you have it in cotton.
  e Do you know the price in roubles?

UNIT 9 Health problems

1 a Office Services
  b bad back pain
  c Accounts
  d fall, and cut on head

2 a neck, shoulder
  b ear, nose
  c call off, cancel
  d cold, sore throat
  e doctor, dentist
  f run down, tired
  g well, healthy

3 (possible answers)
  a He shouldn't be at work.
  b You ought to see a doctor.
  c She shouldn't walk on it.
  d She should put something on it.
  e He should go to hospital.

4 (possible answers)
  a some   **b** some
  c any   **d** any
  e some

5 I'm afraid I have a bad cold and a high temperature. My doctor has advised me to stay in bed.

I'm sorry if this causes you any inconvenience. You can contact me on my mobile. I should be back at work on the 21st.

UNIT 10 Location and layout

1 See audioscript

2 (possible answers)
  a up   **b** to
  c past   **d** under
  e through   **f** after
  g back to   **h** from

3 (possible answers)
  a follow   **b** Come off
  c turn   **d** Go
  e don't go   **f** turn
  g Go   **h** don't take
  i take   **j** Drive
  k go

4 (possible answers)
  a on   **b** next to
  c next to   **d** between
  e above

UNIT 11 The people you work with

1 a He is a used car salesman.
  b He has to maintain the computer
    systems – he is an IT manager.
  c She is a buyer/purchaser for a car
    company.
  d He is a bookkeeper/accountant
    on the purchasing side.

2 (possible answers)
  a don't have to
  b have to
  c don't have to
  d doesn't have to
  e do you have to

3 (possible answers)
  Job titles
  (assistant) production manager
  (deputy) sales director
  office manager
  accounts manager
  (senior) sales assistant
  senior administrator
  deputy director
  assistant manager
  Departments
  the production department
  the accounts department
  the sales office

4 a Who was it from?
  b Who did you leave it with?
  c Who told you?
  d Who does he have to liaise with?

5 a someone/somebody
  b Someone/Somebody
  c anyone/anybody
  d someone/somebody
    (anyone/anybody)
  e anyone/anybody

6 (possible questions)
  a Has he been with the company
    long?
  b Where did he work before?
  c Which company did he work for?
  d Who else works here?

UNIT 12 A tour of the premises

1 a F   **b** T
  c F   **d** T
  e F

2 (possible answers)
  a – Do you mind if I open the
     door?
    – No, of course not.
  b – Do you mind if I have a
     cigarette?
    – No, go ahead.
  c – Do you mind if I post the letter
     tomorrow?
    – No, that's OK.
  d – Do you mind if I leave early?
    – No, that's all right.
  e – Do you mind if I look in here?
    – Yes, I'm afraid it's private.

3 (possible answers)
  a i   **b** iv
  c ii   **d** v
  e iii

4 (possible answers)
  a – Would you like me to send it
     by fax?
    – Yes please. Could you do that?
  b – Would you like me to post it
     for you?
    – That's very kind of you.
  c – Would you like me to show
     you anything else?
    – Yes, please. I'd like to see...
  d – I'd like you to tell me
     something about the company.
    – Right. First …
  e – I'd like you to book a table
     for me.
    – For how many people?
  f – I'd like you to be very quiet.
    – Yes, of course.
  g – I'd like you to show me the
     testing area.
    – Yes of course. It's this way.

5 a V   **b** V
  c CR   **d** V
  e CR   **f** V
  g V
  Notes: fork-lift truck = vehicle with
  two horizontal prongs that can be
  raised or lowered, which is used for
  lifting/moving goods
  bottling plant = factory where
  liquids are put into bottles.

UNIT 13 Graphs and charts

1 meat packaging 73%, cheese 12%,
  sweets 6%, biscuits 5%,
  pharmaceutical industry 3%

2 a hard   **b** quickly
  c easily   **d** slowly
  e slightly   **f** recently

3 (possible answers)
  a I started this job three months
    ago.
  b I haven't seen Uri since this
    morning.
  c Ella has been on the phone for
    the last fifteen minutes.
  d Business has gone well in recent
    months.
  e I have been working in the
    finance department since the
    beginning of last year.
  f I was in Milan two days ago.

4 i (possible answers)
    vertical axis, bar chart, horizontal
    axis, annual sales (chart), sales
    graph
  ii a iii They have increased prices
       by less than 2%.
    b vi Let me show you this
       graph.
    c i Sales reached a peak in
       2005.
    d iv Prices remained stable last
       year.
    e v 5% of our production goes
       to the Far East.
    f ii South America accounts
       for 20% of our exports.

5
  a three and a quarter
  b an eighth
  c three-quarters
  d a third
  e four per cent
  f twenty-one point five per cent
  g nought point six per cent

UNIT 14 Profit and loss

1 (possible answers)
  a 3   **b** 1
  c 2   **d** 0
  e 0/1

2
  a has been
  b has decreased
  c were
  d rose
  e ended
  f (have) recently repaid
  g have got
  h has offered
  i have become

3
  a Have you checked the ledger? ✓
  b I have checked the ledger this
     morning.   ✓
  e We have received the money. ✓
  h She has been very busy this
     morning.   ✓
  i Have you spoken to our credit
     controller?   ✓

4
  a much/a lot   **b** many
  c many/a lot   **d** a lot of
  e many   **f** a lot/many
  g much   **h** much
  i A lot

  Note: take on staff = employ staff

5
  a healthy
  b bank loans
  c debts
  d creditors
  e price
  f market conditions
  g expenditure
  h corner

Notes: to be over budget = to be above the figure anticipated in the budget; to be down on last year = to be lower than last year: turn the corner = move in a new and better direction

6

Analysis of turnover	Current period: 3 months to 31.3 (€m)	Last year: 3 months to 31.3 (€m)
Road haulage	400	388
Boat building	63	60
Furniture	362	378
Supermarkets	213	220

UNIT 15 Invoicing and payment

1
  a Fiona Murch is calling Mr Kloss.
  b Ms Murch has received a letter from Mr Kloss requesting payment for invoice number 12239. She wants Mr Kloss to explain the letter.
  c The invoice relates to a delivery of twenty boxes of RGX components. Ms Murch's firm received the delivery.
  d Ms Murch has not received the invoice.
  e Mr Kloss will send a copy of the invoice. Fiona Murch will arrange a bank transfer as soon as she receives it

  File note for Mr Kloss (possible text) Fiona Murch called in response to my letter. They did not receive invoice number 12239. She confirmed that they received the goods. I agreed to send a copy of the invoice. She will arrange a bank transfer as soon as she receives it.

2 Dear Sir,
  We have not yet received payment of our invoice number 12239. This was due four weeks ago. Could you please transfer the money as soon as possible.
  If you have already paid this invoice, please disregard this letter.
  Yours faithfully
  A. S. Kloss

  Note: was due = was expected

3 (possible answers)
  a I'll transfer the money at the end of the week.
  b I'll send you one in two days' time.
  c He won't be back from lunch till 1.30.
  d I'll invite the bank manager out to lunch.
  e He won't be back in the office till Tuesday.
  f I'll put it on the next bill.

4 (possible answers)
  i a $324m \div 4 = 81m$
    b $14.75 + 19.3 = ?$
    c $5,201 \times 6$
  ii a Sixteen plus seventeen point five minus eight comes to twenty-five point five.
    b Two hundred and thirty-one million multiplied by sixteen and a half.
    c Ninety-three point two per cent divided by four equals twenty-three point three per cent.

5 (possible answers)
  yearly accounts
  a bank balance
  a credit card
  a cheque book
  credit control
  daily totals
  a bank transfer
  monthly instalments
  a bank statement
  weekly deliveries
  payment terms
  a bank account

Notes:

bank statement = printed document from a bank showing the credits and debits on an account and the balance; bank balance = the amount of money in a bank account at a particular time; cheque book = booklet containing new cheques; payment terms = conditions for paying for goods or services, usually specified by the supplier

6 (possible answers)

Sam's corrected notes:

Mary Pick called about invoice no. 29089/1. We invoiced them for 400 sacks, but they ordered 300.
They have received 300 and don't need any more.

ACTION

Send her a new invoice for 300 sacks. Make sure that the sales tax rate is clearly shown on the invoice.

Note: to query an invoice = to ask a question about an invoice, to suggest it is wrong.

UNIT 16 Setting up a visit

1 a iii   **b** ii
  c iv   **d** i

2 a It's going to snow. [F]
    It's snowing. [P]
  b I'm going to learn French. [F]
    I'm learning French. [P]
  c Are you going to work tomorrow? [F]
    Are you working tomorrow? [F]
  d He's going to check the figures. [F]
    He's checking the figures tonight. [F]
  e The company is going to do very well. [F]
    The company is doing very well. [P]
  f Are you going to meet Mike for lunch? [F]
    Are you meeting Mike for lunch? [P]

3 a beginning   **b** difficult
  c following   **d** possible
  e suit   **f** arranged
  g moved   **h** confirmed
  i see if   **j** available

4 (possible answers)
  a How much time do you need to spend there?
  b Which day are you available?
  c Who do you want to see?
  d How many days are you going for?
  e Where do you want to stay?
  f When are you free to meet?
  g What time do you want to meet him?
  h How are you going travel?

5 (possible answers)
  a I would like to set up a visit.
  b Would the 27th be possible?
  c My colleagues would prefer the following week.
  d Would you like to visit the new factory?
  e Would you like a coffee?
  f Friday would be fine.
  g When would you like to come?
  h Would it be possible to change the time?

UNIT 17 Means of travel

1 a two
  b one hour fifty minutes
  c Valence
  d Vienne
  e about 3km
  f the industrial estate

2 (possible answers)
  a The ferry usually arrives at 10.30.
  b The train is not often late.
  c Have you ever travelled by bullet train?
  d He flies to Tokyo once a month.
  e Do you always travel first class?
  f I sometimes drive to work; it depends on the traffic.
  g I have been to Moscow twice.
  h There is never a taxi when you need one.

3 a by train   **b** service
  c How often   **d** every half hour
  e reliable   **f** Change
  g take   **h** Get off

4 a iii   **b** v
  c ii   **d** iv
  e i

UNIT 18 Travel problems

1 a There was no snow in France last week, but there was a lot in Germany.
  b They didn't have much sun in April, and they had none in May.
  c There is no milk left, but there is some cream.
  d There was no rain in August, but there were floods in September.
  e There was a lot of traffic on the road yesterday, but there was none today.

2 (possible answers)
  a It was so cold (that) I had to wear a coat.
  b There was so much fog (that) the plane couldn't land.
  c I was so late (that) I missed the train.
  d There was such a lot of snow (that) I cancelled the trip.
  e It was such bad weather (that) the plane couldn't take off.
  f There were so many delays (that) I couldn't make the meeting.
  g It was such a wonderful day (that) I went to the beach.
  h The traffic was so bad (that) I was an hour late.

3 a so   **b** still
  c the problem   **d** valid
  e to sort out   **f** difficult
  g depends   **h** I'm hoping

4 a icy   **b** flooding
  c foggy   **d** storms
  e hurricane   **f** lightning
  g raining   **h** windy
  i freezing   **j** sun

5 (possible answers)
  a The train is delayed.
  b The plane is fully booked.
  c I've lost my ticket.
  d I missed my connecting flight.
  e My luggage is missing.
  f Your visa is not valid.
  g My passport is out of date

6 a Minus five degrees Centigrade/
    Five degrees below zero
  b Eleven degrees Centigrade
  c Seventy-five degrees Fahrenheit
  d Twenty-eight degrees Fahrenheit
  e Minus fifteen degrees
    Centigrade/Fifteen degrees below
    zero

UNIT 19 About the product

1 Amended memo (suggestion)
  Title: The ERXGU computer
  • The <u>ERXGU</u> computer is €3,500
    including VAT, so it is within our
    budget of €5,000 per machine (I
    didn't ask but I am sure we will
    get a discount if we buy in
    quantity).
  • It would fit the space available at
    most workstations; the base is
    <u>35cm × 25cm</u> – it weighs <u>4.5kg</u>.
  • It comes with <u>a two-year</u>
    warranty – I need to find out in
    more detail what this covers.

2 (possible answers)
  a What is it made of? Could you tell
    me what it is made of?
  b What colour would you like it in?
    Could you tell me what colour
    you would like it in?
  c Which size would you like?
    Could you tell me which size you
    would like?
  d What do you need it for? Can you
    tell me what you need it for?
  e How much does it weigh? Could
    you tell how much it weighs?

3 i a plastic   **b** metal
    c glass   **d** fibreglass
    e wood   **f** paper
    g tin   **h** rubber
    i gold   **j** brass

  ii (possible answers)
    a Packing cases are usually made
      of wood.
    b Tyres are usually made of
      rubber.
    c Cans can be made of tin.
    d Small boats can be made of
      fibreglass or wood.
    e Books are usually made of
      paper.
    f A wedding ring is usually
      made of gold.

4 a length   **b** weighs
  c high   **d** depth

UNIT 20 About the process

1 1 The empty yoghurt pots are
    brought to the filling line by an
    automatic conveyor.
  2 The pots are filled automatically.
  3 The pots are sealed.
  4 The sealed pots are packed in
    boxes by hand.
  5 The boxes are placed on pallets.
  6 The pallets are wrapped.
  7 The pallets are taken to Despatch.
  8 The pallets are loaded onto
    lorries.

2 a We usually keep customers
    informed.
  b We sometimes give gifts to
    customers.
  c We never give gifts to suppliers.
  d We rarely take orders on the
    phone.
  e We still send some orders by fax.

3 a are received   **b** are given
  c are brought   **d** are loaded
  e was asked   **f** was taken

4 Sample instructions for making
    coffee in a cafetière

First, fill the kettle with water and
switch it on. It is important that the
cafetière is clean – it should be
washed if necessary. If the cafetière
is medium-sized, four tablespoons of
fresh ground coffee are then put into
the pot. When the water boils, it is
poured into the pot. It should not
actually be boiling when it is poured.
Next, the top of the cafetière is
replaced. After that, the plunger is
pushed down, and the coffee is
ready to be drunk. In the UK, coffee
is usually served with milk or
cream. Sugar is also added by
some people.

UNIT 21 Making comparisons

1

	price	taste	packaging
Brand A	3	2	2
Brand B	2	1	1
Brand C	1	3	3

2 (possible answers)
  a other   **b** one
  c another   **d** others
  e one   **f** other

3 a Uruguay
  b the Caspian Sea
  c Everest
  d is deeper than
  e is longer than
  f Mexico City

Notes: Everest and K2 = the first and
second highest mountains in the
world; the Nile/Amazon = major
rivers in Africa/Latin America; Cairo
is the capital of Egypt

4 a This company isn't as successful
    as that company.
    It is less successful than that one.
    It is the least successful.
  b This watch isn't as expensive as
    the other watches.
    It is less expensive than the other
    ones.
    It is the least expensive.
  c These lenses aren't as durable as
    those lenses.

They are less durable than those ones.
They are the least durable.

5 (possible answers)

  a shorter, the shortest
  b more economical, the most economical
     uneconomical, more uneconomical, the most uneconomical
  c more interesting, the most interesting
     uninteresting, more uninteresting, the most uninteresting
     (or less interesting, the least interesting)
  d richer, the richest
     poor, poorer, the poorest
  e larger, the largest
     small, smaller, the smallest
  f faster, the fastest
     slow, slower, the slowest

UNIT 22 Arranging meetings/appointments

1 (possible messages)

  a Linda called. She can't make Friday's meeting. She'll be in Berlin at the Richter Hotel.
  b Reza is away until Thursday next week. If you need to speak to him, you can reach him at home (John has the number).
  c Peter Green rang. He's still at the airport, but he should be with you in an hour.
  d Call Rose Wall on 90908. She'll be on that number for two hours. After that, she'll be on her mobile.

2 a should be   **b** leaves
  c arrive   **d** should get
  e I'll call   **f** should arrive
  g leave   **h** have, finishes

3 a by   **b** by
  c for   **d** in
  e until/till   **f** until/till
  g by   **h** for

4 (possible replies)
  Message A
  The Grand Hotel will be fine. Please go ahead and book it.
  Message B
  I'm afraid I can't make it to London next week. I'm away.
  Message C
  I'm afraid I won't be in my office on Wednesday afternoon. Could we meet in the evening?

5 (correct order)
  A: Stubbs Engineering. Good morning.
  B: Good morning. Can I speak to Lucy Stubbs?
  A: Who's calling?
  B: It's Roland Pasquale.
  A: One moment, please ... I'm afraid there's no answer.
  B: Do you know when she'll be back?
  A: She should be back at five o'clock.
  B: Can I leave a message?
  A: Yes, of course.
  B: Could you tell her that Roland Pasquale called about Tuesday's meeting? Thank you.

UNIT 23 Checking programmes and schedules

1 a Jan 16   **b** 10am
  c the hotel   **d** 5.35pm
  e the Regal   **f** TRG inc.

2 (possible answers)
  a anywhere
  b nothing
  c nowhere
  d somewhere
  e someone
  f something/nothing
  g No one/Someone

3 (possible answers)
  a It'll be OK – let me speak to their MD.
  b Did you let everyone go home early?
  c I didn't let them see the plans.

  d Can you let us have the delivery on Thursday?
  e Could you let me know what happens?

4 a number   **b** directory
  c enquiries   **d** listed
  e engaged   **f** busy
  g on   **h** through
  i line   **j** speak
  k text

UNIT 24 A change of plans

1 a He's got a bad back.
  b He can't get a flight.
  c Something has come up.
  d He's had some bad news.
  e He has to go to Paris.

2 a Why doesn't she put the meeting off till next week?
  b Why don't we make it just after three o'clock?
  c Why don't I meet you in a hotel?
  d Why don't we meet on Friday instead?
  e Why don't we send her a 'get well' card?
  f Why don't you take the day off?

Notes: put the meeting off = postpone the meeting; take the day off = have the day as a holiday

3 1 h   **2** a
  3 b   **4** d
  5 c   **6** g
  7 f   **8** e

4 (possible answers)
  a The people called at
     6.50 [✓] 6.58 [✓] 7.00 [ ]
  b He left the hotel at
     7.28 [ ] 7.37 [✓] 7.31 [✓]
  c He reached the office at
     7.55 [✓] 8.05 [✓] 8.10 [✓]
  d Pat arrived at
     7.50 [ ] 8.10 [✓] 8.15 [ ]
  e The meeting finished at
     11.55 [✓] 12.00 [ ] 12.10 [ ]

UNIT 25 Eating out

1 Tuesday 17th February

Name:	Day	Time	Number
Lever	Wednesday	8pm	3
De Haan	tonight (Tuesday)	9pm	2
Gaultier	Friday	7.30pm	4

2 a starters
  b cold drinks
  c kinds of salad
  d meat
  e fish
  f coffees
  g desserts
  h types of fruit juice
  i flavours of ice-cream
  j vegetables

3i (possible answers)
  a a piece/slice of chocolate cake
  b a selection of fruit
  c a cup of tea
  d a box of matches
  e a glass of mineral water
  f a piece/slice of toast
  g a list/range of services

ii (possible answers)
  a – Would you like a dessert?
     – Yes, I'll have a slice of chocolate cake.
  b – Room service.
     – Could you send a selection of fruit to room 47?
  c – What can I get you?
     – I'd like a cup of tea, please.
  d – Can I help you?
     – Yes, a box of matches, please.
  e – Excuse me, I ordered a glass of mineral water.
     – I'm sorry, sir. I'll get it right away.
  f – I had coffee, a piece of toast and an orange juice.
     – That's four dollars fifty.
  g – We offer a range of services.
     – Do you arrange installation?
     – Yes, we do.

4 a either   b either
  c both   d both
  e either

UNIT 26 Leisure activities

1 i The first dialogue relates to the email.
  ii Sample email confirming the arrangements in the second dialogue:

Hi

Good news! I have managed to get two tickets for the AC Milan game on Tuesday.

Why don't we meet at your office? I could drive you to the ground. If the traffic isn't too bad, we could perhaps have a drink before the game.

If I don't hear from you, I'll pick you up from your office just after 6.30.

See you soon.

Sam

2 a So could I. / I could too.
  b Neither/Nor do I. / I don't either.
  c So did I. / I did too.
  d So will I. / I will too.
  e Neither/Nor can I. / I can't either.
  f So did I. / I did too.

3 (possible answers)
  a We used to employ 2,000 people.
  b We used to manufacture the parts ourselves.
  c We used to open at nine o'clock.
  d Our head office used to be in Paris.
  e I used to play football every Saturday.
  f I used to like going to concerts.
  g I used to play in a jazz band.
  h I used to work for LMK.

4 a swimming, sailing, windsurfing
  b football, rugby, American football
  c ballet, theatre, opera
  d boxing, wrestling, judo
  e chess, draughts, bridge
  f jazz, classical, folk
  g detective novels, magazines, newspapers

UNIT 27 Nightlife

1 The second dialogue relates to the thank you letter.

Sample thank you email for the first dialogue:

Thank you for a great night out. I thoroughly enjoyed listening to the bagpipes and I promise that next time I will get up and dance!

When is your next trip to this area?

We don't have bagpipes but we do have hot springs which are fun and good for the health – a bit like Scottish dancing! I would be delighted to take you.

2 a must/has to
  b have to/must
  c mustn't
  d had to
  e have to
  f had to
  g has to/must
  h mustn't
  i have to

Note: We use *must* for immediate obligations and requirements, e.g. I must post this letter. We use *have to* for general obligations and requirements, e.g. I have to wear a suit for work. However, in everyday language the two are often used interchangeably.

3 a a colleague of Mr Fenn's
  b some customers of theirs
  c one of your proposals
  d a suggestion of Tim's
  e one of our advertisements
  f some ideas of his

4 a a few   b a few
  c a little   d a little
  e a little   f A few
  g a little

UNIT 28 The market

1 a ii   b i
  c iv   d v
  e iii

2
a a beautiful new Jaguar
b an experienced Spanish manager
c a large wooden table
d a challenging new market
e an ugly red building
f the old training department
g an expensive Italian leather briefcase
h a medium-sized Swiss manufacturing company

3 (possible answers)
a better
b more efficiently
c later
d harder
e less intelligently
f faster
g more slowly/less quickly
h more aggressively

4
a one/a hundred and three
b one/a hundred and forty-five
c forty-fifth
d twenty-seven thousand, nine hundred and eighty-seven
e four hundred and fifty-six thousand, nine hundred and one
f three million, one thousand, nine hundred and eight
g sixty-five billion
h twenty-third

UNIT 29 Distribution

1
a Mr Martin has been trying to contact Ms Reed all morning.
b He wants to know where Ms Reed has been.
c Ms Reed has (only) just arrived.
d She doesn't know where her colleagues are because she hasn't seen anyone this morning.
e Mr Martin is calling because their order hasn't arrived.
f He spent all day waiting for their truck.
g And he's been waiting for it all (this) morning.
h Ms Reed promises to phone their transport company immediately and to call Mr Reed back in ten minutes.

2
a subcontract
b distribution network
c fleet
d forwarding
e warehouses
f air freight
g rail freight

3
a I've been making phone calls.
b I've been playing tennis.
c I've been arguing with the accounts department.
d I've been moving boxes all morning.
e I've been having lunch with some customers.
f I've been working on some sales figures.
g Nothing, but I haven't been sleeping very well.

4 (possible answers)
a He called this morning.
b He has not received it yet.
c I have been trying to contact the courier since then.
d He has not been answering his phone.
e We have had (We have been having) a lot of problems with our courier service recently.
f Deliveries have been arriving late.
g Deliveries have been getting lost.
h I have decided to end their contract.

5 (correct sentences)
a I've left my car at home today.
b We've been using Framptons quite a lot recently.
We've used Framptons a lot recently.
c I've finished all the paperwork.
I've been finishing the paperwork.
d We've received three of the four parcels.
e Have we heard from the subcontractors?

6 (possible answers)
a No, we don't.
b n/a (not applicable)
c No, we don't.
d Yes, we do.
e We use a local courier.

Sample statement
We don't have our own lorries. We subcontract all our deliveries and transportation. We use a local courier for deliveries under 50 kilometres, and an international company for exports.

UNIT 30 The competition

1 (possible answers)
(see also audioscript)
a Our products are much cheaper.
b Our products are slightly more expensive, but the quality is very high.
c Our support services are the best available.
d We have a very much wider range of customers.
e We are one of the smallest companies in the field, but our technical knowledge is the best in the world.

2 (stress as marked)

compet**i**tor	compet**i**tion	to comp**e**te
prod**u**cer	prod**u**ction	to prod**u**ce
empl**o**yer	empl**o**yment	to empl**o**y
suppli**e**r	s**u**pply	to suppl**y**
distr**i**butor	distrib**u**tion	to distr**i**bute
manuf**a**cturer	man**u**facture	to manuf**a**cture
m**a**nager	m**a**nagement	to m**a**nage
administr**a**tor	administr**a**tion	to admin**i**ster
organise	organis**a**tion	to **o**rganise

3
a are   b is
c are/is   d are
e is   f is
g is   h is
i are/is

4 i (possible answers)
   1 by far the biggest
   2 far bigger
   3 very much bigger
   4 a lot bigger/much bigger
   6 not much bigger/slightly bigger
   8 marginally bigger

UNIT 31 Forecasting

1 1 d   **2** a
   3 c   **4** b

2 (possible answers)
   a choose   **b** will have
   c decide   **d** will have
   e will do   **f** don't offer
   g may lose   **h** isn't offered
   i will offer   **j** will stay
   k doesn't get

3 a Sales decreased.
   b Prices will probably go up.
   c We predict a 10% increase.
   d We expect sales to increase substantially.

4 (possible answers)
   a quarter   **b** half
   c in   **d** summer
   e sales   **f** year

UNIT 32 Trade enquiries

1 a ii   **b** iii
   c i

2 a Have you got enough time?
   b I see I didn't order enough headed notepaper.
   c I don't think we have enough space to store it.
   d Your prices aren't competitive enough.
   e The other model doesn't sell well enough.
   f Our customers don't have enough money to buy products like these.
   g Have you got enough publicity material?

Notes: headed notepaper = writing paper with the name/logo printed at the head/top

3 i The relative pronouns can be deleted in the following sentences:
   b The person you spoke to is not at his desk.
   c The line you want is engaged.
   e The item you ordered is ready for collection.

   ii (possible answers)
   a We are looking for something which/that is economical to run.
   b I'm afraid I can't find the man who/that knows about this.
   c Can you put me through to the department which/that deals with new enquiries?
   d Can I check the details (which/that) you sent to me?
   e Can I speak to the person who/that handles telephone sales?
   f The extension (which/that) you want is engaged.

Note: strong links = strong connections, contacts

4 a who deals with
   b enquiring about
   c on your new range
   d that is both
   e good value
   f a brochure
   g too expensive
   h a price list

Notes: trade enquiries = enquiries from business customers, not the general public; Trade Enquiries = a special section/department that deals with trade customers

5 (possible answers)
   a Not many people agree with me, but I think Teresa might resign.
   b Everyone expects us to get the contract, but I'm not sure.
   c If the parts are delivered late we certainly won't finish the job on time.

d The Democrats are certain/sure to win the next election.
e We're hoping to spend a few days in New York while we're in the States, but we may not have enough time.
f We certainly won't go to that restaurant again.

UNIT 33 Clarification and adjustment

1   YES NO
   a Didn't you order eight?   ✓
   b Isn't the price $8?   ✓
   c Aren't you John Kaye?   ✓
   d Didn't you order CFL 18s?   ✓
   e Didn't you say Tuesday?   ✓

2 (possible answers)
   a I didn't know you would be away when I made the arrangements.
   b OK, I'll make a deal with you …
   c Could I make a reservation for the 25th?
   d Can I make a suggestion?
   e I need to make a quick phone call.
   f We made a slight loss last year.
   g We made some very good contacts in Riyadh.
   h We hope to do more business in South America.

3 a Shall I send you the new model in place of the LS 24?
   b No change.
   c No change.
   d We ordered the green model in place of the blue one.
   e No change.
   f Could you send us three boxes of PL 40s in place of the PL 50s that were delivered by mistake?

4 a in connection with
   b overcharged
   c your records
   d the details
   e According to
   f the unit price
   g out-of-date

5i (possible answers)
I am sorry.
I am very sorry.
I am very sorry indeed.
I am really sorry.
I am really very sorry.
I am really very sorry indeed.
I apologise.
I do apologise.
I really apologise.
I really do apologise.
I am so sorry.
I am really so sorry.
I am really so very sorry.

ii (possible responses)
That's OK.
Really, that's OK.
Don't mention it.
Really, don't mention it.
Please don't mention it.
It doesn't matter.
It really doesn't matter.
Really, it doesn't matter.
Don't worry.
Really, don't worry.
Please don't worry.

6 a = Dialogue 3
  b = Dialogue 2
  c = Dialogue 1
  d & e were not mentioned.

UNIT 34 Making bookings

1 a iii   **b** i
  c iv   **d** ii

2 a musical   **b** box
  c show   **d** rugby
  e wrestling   **f** pitch
  g player   **h** crowd

3 a I will contact you when I have
    the information.
  b If there are no tickets, I will call
    you.
  c I will confirm the booking as soon
    as I get your quote.

  d When the contract is signed, we
    will pay the deposit.
  e I will get back to you if there are
    any problems.

  Note: *I will, you will,* etc are often
  contracted to *I'll, you'll,* etc.

4 a to entertain
  b the main events
  c for the 27th
  d row
  e in the middle
  f include
  g confirm
  h receive

5 (possible answers)
  a I'd prefer to go to the theatre than
    watch a video.
  b I'd rather listen to the radio than
    read a book.
  c I'd prefer to live in the country
    than in the city.
  d I'd rather play tennis than watch
    tennis.

  Note: negative preferences: I'd
  rather not go to the cinema this
  evening. I'd prefer not to go to
  the cinema

UNIT 35 When things go wrong

1 (possible answers)
  a He said there was a mistake at
    their end.
  b She said they had no record of the
    booking.
  c He said they could only offer a
    double room on that date.
  d He said they didn't receive/hadn't
    received the customer's
    confirmation.
  e She said she would confirm the
    booking in writing.
  f He said they were fully booked.

2 (possible answers)
  a The plane is only half full.
  b They will probably change the
    booking if you go to the office.
  c The sales conference will
    probably be in May.

  d The promotions manager also has
    the number.
  e We only have two days left.

3 a iii   **b** v
  c i   **d** vi
  e iv   **f** ii

4 a to   **b** with
  c told   **d** of
  e made   **f** received
  g by

UNIT 36 Sorting things out

1 a The bath needed cleaning.
  b The document needed typing.
  c The cases needed carrying
    downstairs.
  d My suit needed cleaning.
  e The bed needed making.
  i I took it up there myself.
  ii She typed it herself.
  iii He made the bed himself.
  iv They carried them down
     themselves.
  v We cleaned it ourselves

  a v   **b** ii
  c iv   **d** i
  e iii

2 a No, she was reading her mail.
  b She was having lunch.
  c Yes, he was.
  d No, he was writing a report.
  e He was making phone calls.

3 a Where can I get a suit cleaned?
  b Where can I get my shirts
    washed?
  c Where can I get some copies
    made of this report?
  d Where can I get a film developed?
  e Where can I get a letter
    translated?
  i I'm still looking for a dry
    cleaner's.
  ii I still can't find a camera shop.
  iii The laundry isn't open yet.
  iv Do you still have the address of
     the business service centre?
  v I haven't found a photocopier
    that works yet.

a	i	**b**	iii
c	v	**d**	ii
e	iv		

4 (possible answers)

The four promises were:

1 The room would be large enough for the customer's needs.

2 It would be ready for use at 10am.

3 It would be air-conditioned.

4 Refreshments would be served at times agreed with Mr Agit.

Notes: assured me = promised me; will reflect (these circumstances) = will show/coincide with (these circumstances)

Audioscripts

UNIT 1 You and your background

1 Some nationalities and cities

a – Are you from the Munich office?
  – Yes. I was born in Italy, but I've lived in Germany for ten years.
b – Are you English?
  – No, I'm Scottish, but I was born in England. My parents are Scottish, all my uncles and aunts are Scottish. So I'm Scottish.
  – Are you from the Edinburgh office?
  – No, I'm working in Japan, in the Tokyo branch.
c – Are you from the States?
  – Yeah, I am. I'm from New Orleans.
  – Really? What are you doing in Europe?
  – I'm working in the Paris office.
d – You're from Egypt, aren't you?
  – That's right. My name's Heba Saleh. I'm the manager of the Cairo office.
  – Nice to meet you.

UNIT 2 Company structure

1 Names of industries

a Our main business is mining. We're based in Australia. Our head office is in Melbourne. We also have offices in Houston and London. We employ about 200 people. We're part of the MEX group.
b We make computer software. We are a small limited company, based in Pasadena. We are a subsidiary of Excelsior, the computer manufacturer. Their head office is in New York. We have a staff of about 50.
c I work for a large multinational hotels and travel company. I'm on the admin side – I work at our head office in Munich. About 250 people work at our head office, but we employ many more in offices and sites around the world.
d I work in the manufacturing department of ASD. We are a clothing company. We don't sell direct to the public. We specialise in own-brand goods for large retail chains. We are a medium-size company. The manufacturing side is based in Portugal, near Faro.

Notes

Melbourne is in Victoria, Australia; Houston is in Texas, Pasadena is in California, USA. Speaker A is Australian, Speaker B is American, Speaker C is German and Speaker D is Portuguese.

UNIT 3 Company history

1 Milestones

– Were you born in the States?
– No, I was born in Spain. My family comes from Seville in the south. We moved to America in 1983. My uncle was in business there – he had a leather factory.
– Where was he based?
– In Minneapolis. The company was set up in the sixties, but it didn't do very well, so my uncle took over. He bought it quite cheaply.
– When was that?
– In the autumn of 1982. He closed down the shop division, and concentrated on high-quality bags, wallets and belts. Then in 1986, he merged with US Leather and moved his head office to Chicago.
– So business was good …
– It was very good. The company expanded. They took on new staff. By 1995 they employed over 2,000 people.
– When did you join the company?
– When I left college. I worked for my uncle from 1994 to 2004. I worked in the States for three years, then I was sent over to Europe. We opened a European sales office in Madrid. And production was started in Toledo.
– What was your job title?
– I was European Sales Manager.
– Why did you leave the company?
– We were taken over and I lost my job.
– What are you doing now?
– I'm working for PLT Logistics, the distribution company, on the sales side.

UNIT 4 Current projects

1 Work in progress

'We've got three major construction projects going on at the moment. The first is for a hydro-electric power station in Norway. Construction is going very well, and we plan to start up three weeks ahead of schedule, in August.

  'You've probably heard that we are building a brewery in Scotland. The foundations are laid, and building work has started. However, there have been some delays, and we are two months behind schedule. We're trying to make up some time by bringing in extra labour, but we're still having difficulties. Start-up is planned for the spring.

'And then there is the effluent treatment plant which we are building for a Chinese paint factory. This project is going extremely well. It's on target for completion on schedule in January. The company is very pleased with the way things are going, and we are hoping to win a contract to upgrade the effluent plants in their other factories.'

UNIT 5 Meeting a visitor

1 Meeting a visitor

A: Excuse me, are you Otto Ringer?
B: Yes, I am.
A: Hello, my name is Jan Reemik. This is Don Wallis. We're from CET.
B: How do you do?
C: Pleased to meet you.
A: Welcome to London. We're here to meet you and take you to your hotel.
B: That's very kind of you.
A: It's our pleasure. How was your flight?
B: It wasn't too bad.
A: The plane was on time?
B: Yes, it was.
C: Are these your bags, Mr Ringer?
B: Yes, they are.
C: Whose is this carrier bag?
B: That belongs to me too.
A: Right, the car park is this way.

UNIT 6 Introducing your home town

1 Driving to the hotel

A: Excuse me. Can you give me a lift?
B: Yes, of course. Where are you going?
A: To my hotel. I'm staying at the Imperial.
B: That's no problem. I'm going that way …
B: Do you see that place over there?
A: Yes.
B: That's the new exhibition centre, which opened last summer. It's very successful. There used to be a glass factory there, but it was pulled down.
A: What are those buildings?
B: The first one is the town hall, and that's the main library …
A: … Is that the railway station?
B: Yes, that's right. The train service to Geneva is excellent, and there are good links to Eastern Europe from the airport.

A: What's the population?
B: It's just over 1.2 million, I think.

UNIT 7 Chance meeting

1 Greetings and goodbyes

a – It was nice to see you again.
– Yes, It was. Give my regards to Frank when you get back.
– Yes, I will. Thanks for a wonderful evening.
– You're welcome. Good night.
– Good night.
b – I'm sorry but I must leave now.
– Don't worry. It was nice to see you.
– It was nice to see you too.
– Give my regards to your wife.
– I will. See you soon.
– Yes, see you.
c – It was good to see you again.
– Yes. Say hello to John.
– Yeah, I will. Don't forget to send the figures.
– Don't worry – I'll send them.
– Thanks. Give me a ring some time.
– Yes, we must keep in touch.
– So long. See you in September.

UNIT 8 Shopping

1 Buying a pair of shoes

A: Can I help you?
B: I'm looking for a pair of formal black shoes.
A: Can you tell me what size you are?
B: Seven.
A: What's that in European size?
B: I'm not sure.
A: I'll check … You need a size 39. These are your size.
B: How much are they?
A: They're €120 a pair.
B: How much is that in dollars?
A: It's about 150 US dollars.
B: Have you got anything cheaper?
A: What about these? They're €105.
B: Can I try them on?
A: Of course … They suit you.

UNIT 9 Health problems

1 Saying what is wrong

a – Can I come in?
   – Yes, of course. What's the problem?
   – I've got a pain in my back. I can't sit down properly and it hurts when I move.
   – Where does it hurt?
   – I'm not sure.
   – Does it hurt here?
   – Oh! Yes!
   – How did you do it?
   – I was moving a box and I suddenly had this terrible pain. Have you got any pain-killers?
   – Yes, I have, but I think you ought to see a doctor. You certainly shouldn't move more than necessary … I'll call an ambulance. I'm sorry – I can't remember your name.
   – Dan Orbach.
   – You're in Office Services, aren't you?
   – Yes, that's right.

b – Excuse me. Have you got a bandage or something?
   – What happened?
   – I slipped and banged my head.
   – Oh, yes – it's bleeding. Where was this?
   – Outside the storeroom; the floor was wet.
   – Sit down. I'll clean it and put a dressing on it. How are you feeling?
   – A bit dizzy, my head hurts.
   – Can you see all right?
   – Yes.
   – You ought to go home.
   – My car's in the car park.
   – You shouldn't drive. Not for about 24 hours. I'll call a taxi for you.
   – Thanks.
   – I need your name and department for my records.
   – It's Ken Pole. I'm in the accounts department.

UNIT 10 Location and layout

1 Directions

a Come off the motorway and head towards Windsor.
b Take the first turning on the left, and the second on the right.
c Then turn right at the second set of traffic lights. Look out for the building with no windows.
d It's just on the outskirts of town, about six kilometres north-east of the centre.
e We're on a small industrial estate just off the autobahn. You can't miss the building. It's the one with the red roof.

Notes
Windsor = a town in the south of England.
Autobahn (German) = motorway.

UNIT 11 The people you work with

1 Jobs

a I'm in the car business. I'm responsible for all used car sales. We sell about … thirty cars a week.
b I work for a large car company, and it's my job to maintain the computer systems.
c I work for a car company, too. I'm a buyer. I have to liaise very closely with our production people. We try to keep our stocks of components as low as possible.
d I look after all the bills that come into the company. I have to check details of all invoices.

UNIT 12 A tour of the premises

1 A welcoming talk

'If you'd like to take off your jackets, please do. There are some coat hangers over there.

   'We started on this site in 1925. I'll show you a picture of the original buildings in a moment. Our factories are spread throughout the country. We also have plants in France, Spain and in India. We have recently signed an agreement with Bulgaria to build the wings of our aircraft there.

   'This is a plan of the site. If you look here in the corner, you can see where you came in through the main gate. You came past the hangars. We'll have a look at those later this afternoon.

   'Well, if you have no further questions, we can go over and have a look at some aircraft.'

UNIT 13 Graphs and charts

1 Using a pie chart/percentages

'A little bit about our main customer areas. As you can see, the meat packaging industry accounts for a very large amount of our business, 73%. Cheese, although it looks quite a small amount at 12%, is actually very significant here in the home market. We do lots of business with cheese manufacturers. The other areas are confectionery, mainly sweets (6%), biscuits (5%), and pharmaceutical products, medical supplies, etc. (3%). But certainly meat and cheese are our principal business areas. Moving on to our next slide …'

UNIT 14 Profit and loss

1 Business performance

a It was a fairly good year for us. Most of our outlets made a profit, but not all.

b The diamond market was very depressed, and that means reduced profits for us.

c It was a good year in terms of increased turnover, but unfortunately we didn't increase our profit.

d It was a terrible year. One of our biggest customers went bankrupt, and the market for our chicken products collapsed. We lost about $1 million.

e The shipping business was in recession last year and we had to borrow a lot of money. Our loans now total about 25 million Indian rupees.

UNIT 15 Invoicing and payment

1 A missing invoice

– Can I speak to Mr Kloss?

– Speaking.

– Hello, Mr Kloss. My name's Fiona Murch. I've just received your letter concerning invoice number 12239. I'm afraid we have no record of it. Could you tell me what it was for?

– Yes, it was for twenty boxes of RGX components.

– Could you hold on, please? I'll just check our files. Right, I've got the details here. The components have arrived, but there is no sign of your invoice. Could you send me a copy and I'll arrange a bank transfer immediately?

– I'll do that. The post is terrible these days!

Note

Fiona Murch is American. Mr Kloss has a British accent.

UNIT 16 Setting up a visit

1 Time zones/24-hour clock

a – So, when will you call me?

– I'll call you at 15.00 hours your time. That's 09.00 hours our time.

b – Shall I call you when the meeting's over?

– What time will that be?

– I think it'll end at about 3.30 local time. That's 8.30 your time.

– In the evening?

– No, in the morning. We're ahead of you.

c – When does my plane get in?

– At twelve o'clock local time. That's 5pm your time … So you'll have time to call the office before they go home.

d – They are (They're) organising a video conference.

– When is it?

– At 10.30 in the morning – that's their time.

– What is (What's) the time difference?

– We are (We're) five hours ahead of them.

– So the conference would be at 3.30pm.

– Yes. Is that OK?

– Yes, that's fine.

UNIT 17 Means of travel

1 Travel information

– How do I get to the factory?

– Where are you coming from?

– Paris.

– You can come by air or train. Although air is quicker, visitors usually come by train because it's easier. There's an excellent service between Paris and Lyon. The TGV – that's the fast train – only takes an hour fifty minutes. There are two an hour. I don't know the exact times.

– How far are you from Lyon?

– About fifty kilometres. Take the TGV to Lyon Petrache – that's P – E – T – R – A – C – H – E – and then change to the local train to Valence.

– Could you spell Valence?

– V – A – L – E – N – C – E. And get off in Vienne. That's V – I – E – N – N – E. It takes about twenty minutes. We're about three kilometres from the station. There's a taxi rank outside the station. Ask for the industrial estate.

– Thanks very much.

Note

TGV = Très Grands Vitesse (high speed train).

UNIT 18 Travel problems

1 no, none

e.g. – What was the weather like in London last week?

– It was hot, very hot, and sunny.

– Really, in Paris, there was no sun at all.

a – Was there any snow in France last week?

– No, none.

– In Germany there was a lot.

b – We did not (didn't) have much sun in April this year.

– No, we didn't. And in May, we didn't have any.

c – How do you like your coffee?

– With milk, but no sugar, please.

– Oh, there's no milk left. Do you like cream? There is (There's) some in this jug, I think.

d – It was very dry in August.

– Yes, there was no rain at all.

– But there were floods in September.

– Yes …

e – There was a lot of traffic on the road yesterday. I was half an hour late for my meeting. But today the roads were empty.

– Yes, there was no traffic at all this morning. I think there was an accident yesterday, and that's why it was bad.

UNIT 19 About the product

1 A product enquiry
– I'm calling about your ERXGU computer. I have a few questions I'd like to ask you.
– Go ahead.
– First, the price. Could you tell me how much it costs?
– It's €3,500 excluding VAT.
– And how big is it? What's the width of the box? What's the length?
– It's 35cm in length and 25cm in width.
– Thank you. I'd also like to know how much it weighs.
– It's 4.5 kilograms.
– Fine. And what colours does it come in?
– Grey or black.
– OK. Finally, what's the delivery time, and what warranty do you offer?
– Delivery time is usually a week, and the computer has a two-year warranty. Is there anything else you would like to know?
– No, that's fine. You've been very helpful. Thank you very much.

UNIT 20 About the process

1 Sequencing
'First, the empty yoghurt pots are brought to the filling line by an automatic conveyor. They are then filled automatically and sealed. The sealed pots are packed in boxes by hand. Next, the boxes are placed on pallets, and the pallets are wrapped in plastic film. The pallets are then taken to Despatch, where they are loaded onto lorries ready for delivery to the customer.'

Note
The speaker is American and pronounces 'yoghurt' /jəʊgət/; the British pronounciation is /jogət/.

UNIT 21 Making comparisons

1 Comparing brands
'We tested three brands of cheese and these are the results. Brand A was the most expensive. Then Brand B. Brand C was the least expensive. It was much cheaper than the others. In terms of taste, our tester found that Brand B was the best, followed by Brand A. Brand C was the worst. It was very unpleasant. In packaging, too, Brand C did not do well. It was the least attractive. Brand A was less attractive than Brand B. Overall, our tester recommended Brand B. It was far better value than the other brands.'

UNIT 22 Arranging meetings/appointments

1 Taking messages
a Can you tell Markus that Linda called and that I can't make Friday's meeting. I'll be in Berlin, at the Richter Hotel. That's Richter spelt R – I – C – H – T – E – R.
b Please tell Hamid that Reza is away until Thursday next week. If he needs to speak to him, he can call him at home. I'm sure John has the number.
c It's Peter Green here. Could you tell John that I'm still at the airport, but that I should be with him in an hour.
d Could you ask John to call Rose Wall on 90908. I'll be on that number for two hours. After that, I'll be on my mobile.

UNIT 23 Checking programmes and schedules

1 Running through an itinerary
– I'd like to run through the programme with you. Let me know if anything isn't clear.
– Yes, of course.
– So you arrive in New York on January 16th, and we've booked you into Bright's Hotel, 5th Avenue and 55th Street. Their telephone number is 289760 or 734500.
– Right.
– On Monday January 18th at 10am, there's a meeting in our offices with Ben West and Ted Luce of Bison Incorporated. We haven't organised anything for the afternoon yet.
– OK.
– On Tuesday the 19th, we'll send a car to pick you up from your hotel and drive you to Barbara Port at 10am. At 3.30 in the afternoon, a car will take you to Laguardia Airport for your onward flight to Toronto. It leaves at 5.35 and arrives at 7.05. Your hotel in Toronto is the Regal, that's R – E – G – A – L, 59 Avenue Road.
– That's fine.
– We've fixed a meeting with TRG Incorporated for the morning of the 20th, and I'll confirm the names and times later. The afternoon is free.
– OK. Sounds good.

UNIT 24 A change of plans

1 Reasons for not attending
e.g. – Sorry I can't come on Friday. I've broken my leg.
– I'm sorry to hear that.
a – Sorry I can't come on Friday. I've got a bad back.
– I'm sorry to hear that.

b – Sorry I can't come on Friday. I can't get a flight. Why don't we make it Monday instead?
– That's OK by me.

c – I'm very sorry I can't make it on Friday. Something has come up and I can't get away.
– Can you make it earlier in the week?

d – Sorry I can't come on Friday. I've had some very bad news, and I need to stay here.
– Is there anything I can do?

e – I'm sorry, but can we change the date of the meeting? I have to go to Paris on Friday.
– What about next Friday?

UNIT 25 Eating out

1 Reserving a table

a – Can I have a table for three tomorrow night at 8pm, please?
– Certainly, madam. Wednesday at 8pm.
– What name is it?
– Lever.
– Is that L – E – V – E – R?
– Yes it is.
– Thank you.

b – Is it possible to book a table for tonight?
– What time?
– 8.30.
– I'm afraid we have no vacancies at that time. How many people is it for?
– Just two.
– I'll have a table for two at nine o'clock?
– Right, that'll do fine. The name is De Haan. That is (That's) D – E, new word, H – A – A – N.
– Thank you. See you at nine o'clock.

c – I'd like to reserve a table for Friday.
– How many people is it for?
– Four.
– What time do you want the table?
– 7.30.
– That's fine. What's the name please?
– Gaultier. G – A – U – L – T – I – E – R.

UNIT 26 Leisure activities

1 Confirming an arrangement
Dialogue 1
– Are you going to have any free time while you are here?
– I hope so.
– Do you like going to the theatre?
– Yes, but not to musicals. I don't like them very much.
– That's OK. Neither do I.

– I used to enjoy them enormously, but these days I prefer going to things that make you think a bit.
– Well, there's a performance of a new play by a young writer at the National Theatre this week. It's a political thriller. I've heard that it's very good. Would you like to go?
– Yes, that sounds interesting. How about Thursday?
– I'll see if I can get tickets.

Dialogue 2
– Are you free at all this week?
– I'm free in the evenings. I finish work at about 6.30.
– Would you like to go out one evening?
– I'd like to very much.
– Do you like football?
– Yes, I do. I used to watch a lot of football, but recently I've been too busy.
– So have I. I haven't been to a match for a long time. Listen, why don't we go on Tuesday? The local team is playing at home.
– Who against?
– I think its AC Milan. I'll find out what time it starts.
– OK. Let's get some tickets.
– I'll see if there are any left – I'll let you know.

UNIT 27 Nightlife

1 A thank you letter
Dialogue 1
A: That was a wonderful meal, Angus. Thank you.
B: It was my pleasure. It's only nine o'clock. The night is still young. Would you like to do something?
A: Why not? It's my last night. Where shall we go?
B: Do you like Scottish music?
A: Do you mean Scottish dancing?
B: No. There's a place in Aberdeen Street where they have bagpipers. It's nice. We can have a drink. They stay open late; John's a member.
C: But if you want to dance, I'm sure we can find somewhere.
A: No, no, I'd prefer just to listen.
C: Shall we go in your car, Angus?
B: We'd better take a taxi. There's nowhere to park.

Dialogue 2
A: What are we going to do? It's your last night. I think we should do something special.
B: Shall we go to a club or something?
A: I know a place where they have traditional Portuguese music. Would you like that?
B: That sounds great. Where is it?
A: It's near the centre. It's a Fado club.
C: Do you mean that place in the square?
A: Yes, that's the one.

B: Do they serve food, I'm starving!

C: Why don't we go to a restaurant first, and then onto a club afterwards?

B: That's perfect. Is there a cash machine nearby? I'm almost out of money.

A: Don't worry about that, you're our guest.

Notes

Bagpipes = traditional musical instrument played in Scotland.

Fado = traditional folk music of Portugal.

UNIT 28 The market

1 Main markets

a We concentrate heavily on East European markets. We are especially strong in Hungary and Bulgaria.

b Of course, we sell most of our products in Oman and Saudi Arabia. We've managed to increase sales there more successfully than any other parts of the world.

c These days we do a lot of our business in the Far East, the Asia-Pacific area particularly. Japan and Korea are very exciting and important markets for us.

d The States. That's our main market, but we're expanding steadily into Europe as well.

e It's difficult to talk about markets, but we have a lot of business in countries such as Thailand, Laos and Vietnam. We operate mainly in that part of the world.

UNIT 29 Distribution

1 A late delivery

A: Good morning, AR Chemicals. Donya Reed speaking.

B: Good morning. It's Xavier Martin here. I've been trying to contact you all morning, but there has been no one in the office. Where have you all been?

A: I'm sorry Mr Martin, I've just arrived. I'm afraid I don't know where the others are. I haven't seen anyone this morning. How can I help you?

B: It's about our order, reference number 29080. It hasn't arrived. I was waiting for your truck all day yesterday, and I've been waiting for it all morning. Where is it? We need this order urgently.

A: I'm very sorry Mr Martin. I'll call our transport company immediately, and I'll phone you back in ten minutes.

B: Thank you.

UNIT 30 The competition

1 Talking about the competition

a We're certainly a lot cheaper than our competitors. We've concentrated on producing a good quality product at the cheapest possible price.

b Our products are slightly more expensive, but our quality is very high. We have the most advanced systems of quality control in our industry.

c Our support services are by far the best available. We have ten experts who are based in Tokyo, and others in many countries in the world.

d We have a very wide range of customers – I think it's far greater than our competitors. We deal with companies which only employ one or two people, but we also do business with some of the largest multinational companies.

e We are a very small company, probably one of the smallest in the field. We are specialists, and, I would say, our technical knowledge is the best in the world.

UNIT 31 Forecasting

1 Forecasts

a We expect sales to peak in the third quarter of the year. We forecast a sharp fall during the winter.

b The forecast for sales in the short term is very good, but we expect a decline in sales in the longer term.

c We are certain that sales will fall in the short term, but that they will (they'll) pick up in the medium term.

d Profits will rise slowly during the first half of the year, but they will fall back in the second half.

UNIT 32 Trade enquiries

1 Telephone enquiries

a – Can I speak to the person who deals with trade enquiries?
  – Who's calling please?
  – Dave Truck of CLD Cleaning.
  – I'm putting you through.
  – Telephone Sales. How can I help you?

b – Can you put me through to the department that handles telephone sales?
  – I'm sorry sir. You're through to the Head Office here. Telephone sales are at our Reading number. The number is 0297 42017. Hold on, I'll try to connect you.

c – I'd like some information on your new range of phones.
  – The TL 70 range?
  – Yes. Can you send me the specifications? I'm calling from Midway Electric. We're an independent retailer.
  – Sure. Have you got a brochure?
  – No, I haven't.
  – OK. I'll send you the details.
  – Where shall I send the information?
  – Send it to me, Geoff Bordas.
  – Sorry, how do you spell that?

UNIT 33 Clarification and adjustment

1 Negative questions

e.g. – I'll have to order the blue ones for you.
 – Don't you stock the blue ones?
 – No, I'm sorry, we don't.
 – That's OK. I thought you did.

a – We ordered four boxes.
 – Didn't you order eight?
 – Let me check … Yes, you're right. I'm sorry.
 – That's OK.

b – The price is $10 per box.
 – Isn't the price $8?
 – Just a minute, I'll check. No, it's $10.
 – I'm sorry, I thought it was $8.

c – Excuse me. Aren't you John Kaye?
 – Yes, I am.
 – Hello, I'm Jenny Atal.
 – Oh hello. It's nice to meet you again. How are you?
 – Very well, thank you.

d – We ordered three boxes of CFL 9s.
 – Didn't you order CFL 18s?
 – Let me check. No, our purchase order says CFL 9s.
 – I'm sorry. That's our mistake. I'll send you a credit note.
 – Thanks.

e – When are you delivering? It's Monday.
 – Didn't we say Tuesday?
 – No, we said Monday.
 – I'm sure you said Tuesday.
 – Let me check. Oh, yes, you're right.

UNIT 34 Making bookings

1 The Simple Present tense for timetables

a – The play begins at 7.30. The interval is usually at 8.30.
 – What time does the performance end?
 – Usually at about ten o'clock.

b – What time does the film start?
 – At eight o'clock. The show starts at eight and the film itself starts at 8.30.
 – And what time does it finish?
 – At quarter past ten.

c – Do you know when the match begins?
 – They usually start at 2.30. The game is an hour and a half with an interval of 15 minutes.
 – So it ends at about 4.15?
 – Yes, that's right.

d – When does the train leave?
 – It leaves at 14.00. It stops in Swansea at 15.20.
 – When does it arrive?
 – 16.20.
 – It's a fast service.

UNIT 35 When things go wrong

1 Reported speech

e.g. There are no vacancies in first class on Friday's flight.
a There was a mistake at our end.
b We have no record of the booking.
c We can only offer a double room on that date.
d We didn't receive the customer's confirmation.
e I'll confirm the booking in writing.
f We are fully booked.

UNIT 36 Sorting things out

1 Reflexive pronouns

a The bath needed cleaning. We phoned the reception desk several times, but nobody answered. In the end, we had to clean it ourselves.

b She had a document that needed typing. As the business centre wasn't open, she borrowed a laptop and typed it herself.

c Their cases needed carrying downstairs. They were in a hurry because they were late, so they carried them down themselves.

d My suit needed cleaning. I asked the dry cleaner on the second floor to collect it, but no one came. In the end, I took it up there myself.

e He called reception and told them that the bed needed making. They said someone would come right away. But he waited an hour, and nobody came. He was tired and he wanted to go to bed, so he made the bed himself.